PHILIPPINE REBEL STORIES

COLONEL DENNIS V. ECLARIN

Also by Colonel Dennis V Eclarin

Scout Ranger War Stories
Philippine Jungle Survival
Scout Ranger Combat Leadership
Scout Ranger Combat Guide
Scout Ranger Registry
Scout Ranger Memories

Contact the author at
email: dennis_eclarin@yahoo.com

INTRODUCTION

My life's path has been inextricably linked with those of rebels. In 1983, at the height of the insurgency, rebels had threatened our town in Cagayan so that living there became too risky. Our entire town seemed to have been under the influence of rebels already. My family decided that I should accept scholarship at the Philippine Science High School in Diliman. Our entire family gradually moved to Manila after that.

I was in my third year in high school when the EDSA revolution occured in 1986. I saw myself walking the length of the highway just to take a look at the rebel soldiers who were then idolized by the people for their courage.

Inspired by that experience, I considered a military career, and off I went to the Academy two years later.

I was in my first year at West Point when the failed 1989 coup d' etat led by the Scout Rangers happened. I had mixed feelings about the four-day siege of Makati's central business district. While I lamented the loss of lives and property, I was fascinated by the sheer bravery of the rebellious Scout Rangers. I visited them in detention on my first trip home, to tell them that I also wanted to become a Scout Ranger. They later became my mentors in combat.

While the First Scout Ranger Regiment was a combat-oriented unit, I also had memorable non-combat experiences, one of which was when a group of twenty two guerillas surrendered to my team, one by one, over a period of 6 months. Illiterate and unpolished, they appreciated our gesture of helping them with their livelihood. As a gesture of trust, they turned over twenty six of their firearms which they carefully stashed in a lubricant-filled container in the jungle. I soon deeply connected with the low-ranking rebels, whose families had been the real victims of insurgency. They joined the rebellion because of the sheer power of the propaganda that sold them hope. Most of them stayed because they waited for the promises to be fulfilled. They left because the rebel movement failed to help them. In the end, as you will read in this book, most say that becoming a rebel was a wrong decision.

Except for the triumphant EDSA uprising, the pattern of regret over the failure to grasp the true price of rebellion is apparent in all the stories featured in this book, most especially in the story of my friend, Captain Milo Maestrecampo, who was one of the key leaders of the Oakwood Hotel siege in 2003. The sense of repentance shows in the stories of the senior rebels who had witnessed the rise and fall of guerilla fronts under their command. The feeling of being unwitting victims of the revolution is strong, apparent in the gripping personal stories of the women warriors. The deep sense of regret is likewise present in the narratives of the young, teenage rebels who lost the glory of youth with their unplanned involvement in the rebellion.

I have also been a participant in the transformation of a number of our military rebels who desperately tried to rebuild their lives and careers after their detention.

For all the people whose lives had been directly or indirectly affected by the insurgency, I dedicate this book. Many lives had been lost, and many families had been shattered because of the history of conflict in our country. May this book remind us of the high price that we must be willing to pay for a bold decision to become a rebel. I featured rebels from the different groups and across generations to make this point.

I wish to acknowledge the former rebels who shared their personal stories for this book. I have tried my best to accurately capture their truest voices through their stories of hope, struggle and transformation.

COL DENNIS V ECLARIN

Contents

Contents

Wasted Years

I left home when I was only sixteen years old. I went home nine years later, to a crying mother who had always believed that I was already dead. What I experienced in the period of my life is too painful to remember but very hard to forget. I want to share my story because I wish to warn other young ones who have not seen defeat and failure. They are often the easiest to fool. I was a fool nine years ago.

I grew up in a very secluded village frequented by the rebels. There were eleven of us siblings and our father hardly had any food to put on the table. I knew that life was hard because two of my siblings died of malnutrition. Since the rebels always came to our house, I gradually imbibed their teachings. They blamed the government for everything. According to them, my family was poor because the government was inept. Before I could even finish high school, I already hated the government.

The rebel recruiter said my life was hopeless.

"Even if you finish college you won't get a job," she said. She could not finish elementary school, yet she seemed sure of what she was saying.

"Jobs only go to the friends of the people in government," she continued. I believed her.

The following day, I left home before my parents awoke. They did not hear from me nor seen me until nine years later.

I went through all the traumatic experiences any woman could ever go through.

Women like me were supposed to be treated with respect. What happened to me was the opposite.

I cannot say I am beautiful, but I seemed to have attracted the stares of the men. In my first unit, I was the only woman member and boy, they feasted on me. When I was taking a bath in the river, there would be peeping toms behind the bamboo and the bushes. They offended me, but I was alone and defenseless.

There were clear guidelines as to how women warriors were supposed to be treated, but these were all violated to satisfy their fantasies.

One time, a group of my fellow recruits came as I took a bath and sexually molested me. They touched my private parts and though I protested, I was too powerless against them. I complained to our political secretary about my experience. Instead of coming to my defense, he said "Our cadres also have their weaknesses."

"They are not perfect. Just keep silent," he advised me. I kept silent after that, but my womanhood had clearly been violated. I no longer had a father to defend me.

I wrote my mother, telling her that I already miss her. My family was really kind and loving I did not want to leave them, but I somehow believed what the rebels promised me that my parents will get a better life. On my first year, it came to a point where I sorely missed my family. I asked permission to take a leave but my commander promptly turned it down. My letters never reached my parents, and I only found that out when I returned to them nine years later.

I turned seventeen on my second year in the movement.

There was a rapist that the masses brought to us. At that time, I was regarded as a young woman who still felt pure despite the malicious advances of my fellow rebels.

"You must overcome your fear of firing a gun," explained my commander.

"To conquer your fear you must experience killing a person," he continued. I was trembling as he told me this, in front of everybody.

"Kill him with a knife," he said. I was shocked.

I resisted but my commander would not hear of it. I nearly went crazy when I was forced to thrust the knife into his neck, towards his heart.

"Please do not kill me. I won't do it again. I also have a child.

What will happen to my child?" he pleaded.

He died in my hands. And that nightmare stayed with me for several years.

Just like my fellow child warriors, I lost my youth as a rebel.

I felt I lost my youth soon after. While my contemporaries enjoyed their freedom, I was trapped inside the rebel movement. Unlike my friends in the outside world, I cannot play, I cannot go wherever I wanted. I cannot watch movies or sing in karaoke joints. All we did in the mountains was talk, kill, kill and kill some more. I realized that I made a wrong decision, one that cost me my youth — and my future!

In the following years, there were several times when my group figured in fire fights. Throughout most of these, I was shocked and numbed by the violence. Then they said there is no God, but I found myself praying to God.

In one firefight, our leaders practically abandoned us. We expected our leaders to be brave and fight alongside us. But they left us in the battlefield, desperately trying to fend off the attacks of the soldiers. Some of our comrades died, and the other casualties, we could not save because we were all by ourselves. We were like chicks left alone by the mother to survive. Many more clashes against the Army happened after that, and the same thing happened again and again. Our leaders left us when we were most vulnerable.

I was just too young and perhaps too naive. I was traumatized by all the violence that I went through. I saw my companions drop dead one by one. As time passed, I began to wonder how many more were like me.

I had many firsts in the movement. My first relationship was with a fellow fighter. I was turning twenty when I experienced my first love. He was a fellow fighter and I knew it was for real — but it was ill-fated as he died in an armed clash eight months later. That was the first time I lost a loved one.

In a simple ceremony like this, I married the rebel boy of my dreams.

I fell in love once more. This time, I got pregnant. But I had a miscarriage in the middle of a firefight. As my comrades were busy fighting back, I was weeping for the child I lost. That experience haunts me until now.

In my letters to my parents, I tried to present a rosy picture of what was happening to me. Of course, I did not know that all my letters were read by our commander. They never reached my family.

But deep inside, I wanted to share my experiences with any young person who would care to listen. My conscience deeply bothered me because if I did not speak up, more young women can become victims like me. While I had the voice to finally speak out, it was not the right time to do so. I was still in that cage called the revolution. I desperately wanted out, but I did not have the courage to leave.

My salvation came when I was captured by the police. At first I acted wildly, afraid I would be tortured. But I was treated so nicely that it only took a few days of kind treatment by the Army and the police when I realized that they were not bad men after all.

Now, I am back with my family. I have asked my parents for forgiveness. I have strengthened my faith in God again. And with every youth that I meet who is being targeted by the rebels for recruitment I secretly whisper. "Do not make the same mistake I did."

Marilyn De Los Santos
Rebel in Rizal in 2005

A True Revolutionary's Frustrations

I made my first kill a few days short of my fifteenth birthday. It was a cold-blooded assassination of a policeman who was then all by himself by the roadside. I was nervous as I pulled the trigger on the pot-bellied law enforcer. With my first shot, he fell limp, near dead gasping for dear life at the pavement. I fired ten more bullets into his head and chest, near his heart. We left him there, as if swimming his own blood.

My succeeding hits were much easier after that. Our mission was to liquidate politicians and rich people who were against the revolution. We would be deployed as small groups of three to five highly-trained assassins. We specialized in cold-blooded murders in cities and town centers. A target would come from church on a crisp Sunday, and we, the young assassins, would get near him. And in full view of his family and other church goers, we would liquidate him. We remained unaffected by the terror on the faces of the people as we casually walked away from the gruesome scene — the wife crying hysterically and the children unable to understand why their dear father was killed. Most of our victims had children who were too young to understand that their fathers were sacrificed for the revolution.

We also prioritized the killing of businessmen who would not pay revolutionary tax. We would first request a target to pay the revolutionary tax. Every honest entrepreneur would silently resent at the double taxation. He was being taxed by the official government and taxed even heavier by our shadow government. If he did not pay up, our other groups would harass him, his family or business — burn his truck, bus or jeep or threaten his children at school. Most complied with our demands immediately. But if they still held firm, we were sent in to kill them. This was a specially gruesome role. On my second year as an assassin, I had several hits under my belt.

We trained female assassins to assist us.

Orders to liquidate military officers while they were on vacation proved more difficult than executing unarmed, untrained and helpless businessmen.

Though the Geneva Convention expressly prohibited harming combatants on vacation, we were still ordered to kill as many as we could, especially those who caused the guerilla movement heavy casualties.

We felt it was treacherous to do so but we had to follow orders, lest we are suspected of being the military's deep penetration agents.

It was particularly dangerous at that time even for loyal and reliable killers like myself to be under suspicion as it meant certain death.

At age 18, I was already a squad leader of the dreaded Sparrow Unit. To have risen to that rank so quickly, I must have showed the courage and coldness expected of true assassins. But my conscience had begun to bother me.

I was bothered by our mission to kill suspected military agents because all we needed to execute was a small unverified tip that a person was an enemy of the revolution. There was no proof needed. We were not allowed to ask questions, much more hesitate to kill. It was tough to execute a person when it was not clear what his fault was. Even I, a ruthless executioner at that time, found such executions questionable, even unconscionable. We were slowly being regarded as human rights abusers. In my third year as a rebel, I knew it was just a matter of time, when we would lose the sympathy of the people whose support we valued.

I had to leave that unit when I got hit on the chest by a group of policemen in a firefight. It would have been fatal, but perhaps bad people like me are given a second chance to mend our ways. I became a senior training staff at the largest rebel training camp in Northern

Luzon at that time – in the remote jungle fortress called Paco Valley. I welcomed the change of pace. In my previous work, I felt that I was losing my revolutionary fervor, my lofty dreams of becoming a big part of the rebellion. I simply wanted to renew myself.

We trained hundreds of willing recruits with our tactics.

In that place, we gathered recruits from four provinces – Ilocos, Cagayan, Kalinga and Apayao. I do not know if they were coerced but all I know is that at the height of the insurgency in the early 1960's, there were thousands of them. There were 120 people in each batch. A huge number was needed to fill up the rebel ranks in the 1980's. Feeding the trainees was actually the biggest challenge. Back then, much of the rebel resources came from logging companies in the area. If they did not pay, we would burn one or two of their bulldozers and trucks, thereby disrupting their operations. But even while we had money, it was much harder to physically bring rice to our secret training camps. We consumed at least 3 cavans of rice daily and the steady stream of our former couriers bringing in rice to pre designated pick up points always alerted the military. Military operations that cut off our supply lines, interrupted our training. We transferred to the most ideal guerilla haven one can imagine: Marag Valley. The area provided natural protection from attacks: dense forests, tall mountains and a wide river surrounded the valley.

Our defense strategy was simple: we posted snipers along the river banks to guard against military forces attacking from the river. We riddled the mountains and all possible approaches with booby traps and outposts. Inside the village, we restrained the civilians from moving out. They were our human shields against helicopter rocket attacks and howitzer fire missions. Fear of collateral damage prevented military commanders from launching massive artillery attacks.

At Marag Valley, we were able to plan our attacks and prepare for the final strategic counter-offensive against the government forces. According to our doctrine, this was one of the final stages before we could finally claim victory. But we were wrong.

In our desire to increase our ranks, we just accepted whoever volunteered. Many came in because they wanted to avenge the death of family members. Others got in because they just wanted the power of the gun. We wanted those who believed that the revolution can change their lives by giving them a job, education and justice. But we what got were mostly petty thieves and small-time criminals running from the law. Unlike true revolutionaries, they had a strong motivation to stay with us because the only other option would be to go to jail. Some of our recruits would slaughter water buffalos that were left the fields by the farmers whose lives depended on these animals. They would demand chickens from the poor natives, never paying a single cent for these. They would point a gun at a small store owner who refused to give them soap or toothpaste. We were becoming a band of bandits fast, no longer the idealistic revolutionaries that we all claimed to be. I was increasingly frustrated because I was losing my sense of purpose. By that time, I already had a wife and kid to support. I aired my frustration in an open forum among the top 300 hundred rebel leaders in Northern Luzon. I rarely spoke my mind because I had always been seen as a brave rebel field commander.

"You told us that you would support the families of our fighters," I started.

"Yet the monthly allowance you promised remains a dream to most of us who are in the field," I continued. I voiced out against the leaders, who mostly came from their air conditioned safe houses in the cities. They were feeling uneasy in their chairs.

"You told us, that we would be a clean and incorruptible organization, yet we do not see where all the revolutionary taxes are going," I continued. I knew the peasant fighters like me, identified with what I was talking about. But they knew that I was treading on very dangerous ground. It was easy to critique each other after the conduct of our tactical offensives. Having an experienced field commander like me openly question the use of funds was probably hard for the corrupt.

"We are starving here in the field," I continued.

"Some of our fighters even use their guns to extort money and food from the very people we claim to represent," I bravely declared.

I did not mind the tension that everyone in the venue felt. I deserved to air my gripes. I had already served the revolution so faithfully for fifteen years.

I thought I was going to be summarily executed after that meeting. Instead, the leadership put me on restriction, with no command responsibilities, until I was reformed. I lost faith soon after that. I left my firearms and headed home. It was such a painful homecoming after several years in hiding. My parents and my young family were moved to our evacuation center. And what I thought to be our home was gone, demolished. I hugged my wife, my mother and my child. I finally found the sweetest embrace in the evacuation center. I was home and regardless of my violent past, I still had a family that loved me.

I found comfort in my family after years living the guerilla life.

What happened afterwards was unprecedented. It was aired over the radio that I had availed of the Presidential Amnesty as part of the government peace and reconciliation program. I even talked over the radio that I was treated well, so unlike the propaganda inside the movement that we will all be killed if we gave up.

Many more did the same. We gathered them and helped them avail of cash assistance from the government. Their faces showed relief, as their ordeal was finally over.

One of the rebel quartermasters came down. He revealed the arms cache of at least two hundred rifles, machineguns and mortars left by fighters like me. Perhaps motivated by the cash reward, he led government troops to the main arsenal of firearms of the revolution in Northern Luzon.

I spent my youth building the revolution but was later overcome with frustration. In my effort to end this frustration, I also helped cause the revolution's sudden doom.

Ernesto Belen
Top rebel commander in Luzon
in the 1990's

I Just Want a Cow

I am tired of war. War has been a way of life since my youth in the early 1970's. I witnessed the growth of the Muslim Independence Movement since the late 1960s. The royal families led the fight for an independent country. This movement later became the Moro National Liberation Front (MNLF) which was led by a fiery University of the Philippines professor from Sulu. He had many ready recruits among us.

Most of us were barely out of our teens. We did not fully understand what independence was or how we could benefit from it. All we knew was that we were fighting the Christian vigilantes called the Ilagas – whom we all perceived as guardians of the lands that we supposedly owned. Our only aim then was to protect our communities and families from these Christian vigilantes.

Things took a turn for the worse when the MNLF leadership alleged that we were being persecuted because of our religion. Our leader immediately got the attention and support of sympathetic Islamic countries, which provided arms, logistics and money for us to wage a major civil war.

I was a willful participant of that civil war from the early 1970's until the late 1980's when things began to ease up a bit. I was a motivated *mujahideen* who fought for religion, regardless of the consequences to me and my family.

I was a faithful warrior. Then I caught the eye of the one of the spiritual leaders of the Moro National Liberation Front, Hashim Salamat. Quiet and with a gentle demeanor, he was a folk hero. Educated in Egypt as a scholar, he was a fundamentalist. When the Moro National Liberation Front entered into a peace agreement with the Philippine government in the 1990's, Salamat broke away and established the Moro Islamic Liberation Front (MILF). I was one of his early field commanders.

We fought the ferocious Scout Rangers in the 1970's and 1980's.

At that time, Muslims in Central Mindanao idolized us,

their fighters. Everyone that we knew of claimed to be an MILF member. Even the women became fighters. This fervor intensified when we started staking our territories in the major camps that we occupied. We had camps in Lanao del Sur, in Maguindanao and in Sultan Kudarat. But our jewel was the sprawling complex in Barira, Maguindanao that we called Camp Abu Bakar.

I was the battalion commander of our unit that defended our camp and our dear leader. I was such a trusted member of the inner circle of our separatist organization because of the loyalty I had shown in almost three decades of fighting up until that time. But in 2000, when the President of the Republic declared an all-out-war against the thousands of our fighters, we defended our territories with everything that we had.

We would pray in our foxholes, and call for the protection of Allah.

"Let us die in battle, because we will go to heaven," I exhorted my subordinates, and true enough, I have had close calls with death. In one instance, a mortar round fell two meters from me. It exploded and I was thrown a few meters back. I felt numb at first and I thought I lost my feet. I jumped and then I felt my feet again. Nothing hit me, not even a splinter. That is when I said, if Allah does not will it, it won't happen.

I fought even more gallantly after that. The Scout Rangers and the Philippine Marines were our real ground combat opponents. We would not have given up after a few months of fighting had not the government used its bombers and howitzers. We dreaded the kamikaze attacks of the fearless bomber pilots who dropped hundreds of bombs into our locations.

Hundreds among us died because of the endless bomb runs and

creeping howitzer fires. We still had ammunition, and Allah was up there protecting us, but the relentless advance of the soldiers was too strong. We splintered into different directions. I ended up hiding in a nearby province for a few years. Because of the blood debts I owed the government troops, I feared for my life if I surfaced.

"The soldiers are better now," I was assured by my cousin when he started persuading me to come out and formally surrender.

We were worn out warriors when we started coming down for good.

"They won't hurt you," he further assured me. I was full of doubt because throughout my life I had seen firsthand how constabulary men could abuse their power because of Martial Law. They would get our chickens, cows and water buffalos. They would butcher our most prized possessions, which were essential to our livelihood, right in front of our eyes. They hurt us, males who they suspected of being separatists. At that time, almost all of us in our community were rebels.

Eventually, I was persuaded to meet the Army brigade commander in my province. I was tired of hiding and knew I was growing old. I wanted to give up life as a rebel while I still had the energy to start a new life.

"What support do you want, commander?" the Army leader asked me.

He was taken aback by my curt reply.

"I just want a cow sir," I replied to him. My answer surprised him because the cost of what I had asked for was merely a fraction of the large sums of money spent in howitzer rounds and other ammunition.

It must have seemed so cheap to him, but what he did not realize was that a cow was all that mattered to me.

I actually wanted a tractor but a cow was enough. With a cow, I could till the land and plant corn. With my corn harvest, I could finally feed my family.

Nothing much happened in my life since I joined the armed struggle in the early 70s. I do not condemn the revolution nor the Islamic Organization I was once so proud of. But I soon learned that joining the revolution prevents one from taking care of his family.

I wanted to rebuild my life because I sacrificed the future of my children. I had no regular income from my rebel leadership post. But I had to feed my family, send my kids to school and keep them healthy. I was unable to fullfill my responsibilities as a father because I was always gone, always serving the revolution. Something had to change, if I wanted to give my children a better future.

"I do not want any more conflict," I proudly declared to myself. For a true-blue fierce warrior, that was just like giving up what I lived for: kill enemies.

"There is nothing to gain from conflict," I announced to my family. Throughout those years, they had been waiting for me to realize this. They silently thanked Allah for my change of heart.

I felt convinced there had to be an end to the conflict.

My transformation was not easy because I had to undo and unlearn a lot of the attitudes and skills that had made me successful in the battlefield. While I was trained to destroy enemies, I now had to focus on more positive and productive endeavors.

I became more creative in tapping my productive energies. I

focused on making a decent living for my family. I kept my family alive and well entirely from the fruits of my labor. I soon realized that it was truly easier to demand revolutionary taxes from the people than it was to honestly earn money for my family. It was a challenge that I accepted in exchange for the peace that I now enjoy.

Since I started working again as a regular farmer, I have gone on to inspire my former comrades to lay down their arms as well. They too had resumed their once productive profession of farming.

I long for the day when all of my men will have their own chickens and water buffalos, or hopefully, our own tractors. One does not demand these things from the government as resources are limited.

That is why I get anxious whenever a former comrade decides to lead a normal life.

Tempers are volatile and frustration or discontent may push them back to their old ways.

After all, the only way to make sure that he embraces peace is to

I long for the day when all the fighting will stop and we can lead normal lives.

provide sustainable livelihood to feed himself and his family. At the end of the day, every rebel, no matter how hard-core, is primarily a family man.

It has been a few years since I embraced a life of peace and I will never forget that moment when I told the Army commander that all I wanted was a cow for my livelihood.

Peace can be bought cheap. Even if each rebel asked for a cow, the total cost would still be lower than buying the same number of bombs. Bombs kill and maim while cows — and even tractors — can help rebels lead peaceful lives.

Sultan Hassanal Gampong
Former MILF battalion commander

To Serve The People

I live a few hundred meters away from the sprawling Philippine Army Training camp in Capas, Tarlac. Every day, I see young soldiers going through tough training. There are those who, I assume, are training to become officers. These are the enthusiastic idealists. I learned that this newly-built camp churns out most of the junior Army officers — replacements that bring in fresh blood. It is like an assembly line of soldiers that goes on and on until there is no more need for them. But I know this is unlikely because they would need more as long as the insurgency continued.

I was one of the first seven persons that set in motion the outlawed New People's Army in 1969, more than four decades ago. It was a breakaway group from a previous rebel organization that has since then earned a bad reputation because of alleged extortion activities near the American military bases. A young professor from the University of the Philippines had plans of advancing the revolution nationwide. While he had a strong intellectual base among his fellow professors and students, he did not have the brawns that we had. His core following were students who felt threatened with arrest because of their covert revolutionary activities. Their motivations were different from ours.

In my case, it was not ideology or some romantic notion of sweeping social reforms that forced me to become a rebel. Mine was simply for survival. I was charged with assassinating a governor in my province, Tarlac. With my imminent arrest and incarceration, I had to save myself. That was the only reason I joined the revolution. I stayed on for 20 years until I my capture in 1989. I was the chairman of the NPA Military Commission at the time of my arrest.

Upon his capture, I succeeded Commander Dante, center, as the military chief of the New People's Army.

I loved the revolution in the early days. While I joined it for practical reasons, I soon identified with the causes that our small group espoused. I came from a very poor farming family, and I knew what mattered most to the tenant farmers. They just wanted a bigger share of their produce. In our part of the Philippines, feudalism really existed. Big landlords owned the land. Tenant families like us had no choice but to accept the grossly unfair sharing arrangements of the landlord. We were given all the farm inputs like seeds and fertilizers but we had to split the rice produce 50-50 between him and our family — after all the farm inputs and post harvest processing expenses have been deducted. That left a farmer family fed for a few months, so he is forced to advance his share for the next harvest. We had the most willing recruits among the fathers who felt that the only way they could get out of perennial misery was to reclaim the land they tilled afer a victorious revolution. They actually believed then that we can win. Most died or left our underground movement without realizing that dream.

I am not aware if the other members of the group I belonged to intentionally made promises that would keep the people interested in our cause.

I loved organizing the people in the villages. Unlike the students and other intellectuals who joined us, I truly belonged to the oppressed. And, with the power that came with my gun, I tried to do what was best for my fellow farmers.

I tried helping them out by playing the role of an agricultural technician, just like government field workers. With my rifle slung over my shoulder and brimmed hat, I taught the ignorant farmers the different varieties of seeds. I taught them how to take care of rice plants and how to ward off pests. I felt so fulfilled organizing farming communities in teams so that they could help each other out. That, to me, was the beauty of socialism: every person becomes responsible for everybody else's welfare. Yet, there was a "Big Brother" who merely commanded us to be productive, rather than help us out.

Having been a victim of injustice myself, I enjoyed the power we wielded whenever we took the settlement of disputes into our own hands. When a person was accused of robbery, I would organize a "people's court" with a jury composed of villagers. We would hand out a punishment, usually death. That was not easy, especially with their families pleading for mercy, but I had to do it, in the name of the revolution, so we do not lose face and the people's faith in us. I did it so many times, but discomfort never left me. I was a main figure in the young insurgency and I had to do it. Ironically, I was in the same position because I was also accused of a crime I did not commit.

There were many times that I almost died, too. One time, a comrade and I were attacked by a policeman who was tipped off by someone. We downed two of our attackers. I took all these in stride. I had become a veteran and my instincts were honed by experiences like these. But the one thing that bothered me was the disloyalty that slowly spread among our members.

It took years, but everything soon became clear. The military successfully planted deep penetration agents within our ranks. All the attacks on our most secret camps were well-planned. The ambuscades seemed to indicate that the government troops received up-to-date information on our whereabouts. It seemed as if they could even predict our movement. The arrest of the top-ranking leaders and field commanders were even more devastating. With each capture of rebel cadre who had been with the movement for a long time, years of revolutionary experience would be gone, and we would start all over again. These successful military actions on our organization severely devastated the movement.

Before long, paranoia set in. While we were trained to trust each other during the most dangerous times, we soon started becoming suspicious of one another. We controlled all instructions with family members. We closely monitored doubtful actions of our comrades. Then we started the purge.

We were soon so suspicious of each other that we monitored even the most personal communications.

That was when we imploded. Having been a pioneer in organizing different regions, I was trusted by leadership to do the troubleshooting of guerilla fronts under threat. I was sent to Bicol first, where there had been so many rebel deaths in the hands of the military. There were suspected traitors or infiltrators in their ranks. They were right but their local rebel leadership did not know who these were. In desperation, the commanders in the area starting killing their own people — men, women and even their teen recruits - and putting their corpses in mass graves.

"Do not kill anybody without blood debts," was my main order. The executions seemed maniacal already. Anyone who had relatives — close or distant — in government, especially the military, was summarily executed. Anyone with previous links with security forces like the police or the militia were killed with a single shot at the back of the head.

Even our most longtime cadres were suspected of treason.

These events were so demoralizing. Suddenly, even senior members who have been with the movement left and surrendered. They feared for their lives. And I understood why.

"If he can be reformed, do not kill him. Just return him to his family," was my order to remedy the implosion in our ranks. I do not know how our movement recovered because I was captured a few years after that. Was I also turned in like my comrades? I never bothered to find out. At the time I was captured, I was already in my 20th year in the movement. I was the last among the original seven NPA founders to be cornered. At that time, I was the rebel military chief, a lofty rank to attain for a poor farmer who was just escaping justice.

After several years of trying to bring normalcy into my life, I found solid rhythm in becoming a barangay captain of the very same village where we founded the New People's Army in 1969. And despite my long years dreaming the great shift in the way the country's political, social and economic system works, I discovered the pure joy of accomplishing little things. I first had our small village chapel renovated. Despite my long years of preaching a Godless ideology, I was still piously devout. It really dawned on me that our common faith binds us in the most trying circumstances.

I went back to farming after three decades with the revolution.

As the village chief, I also went back to my first love: farming. While I had been used to collecting revolutionary tax even from legitimate businessmen, this time I begged and pleaded. It took several years for my dream project to come true. But when it did, I felt complete. Indeed, that irrigation canal was what the people needed most.

I am now in the twilight of my years. On a few occassions, I meet fellow rebel pioneers and supporters. I would often be asked about the revolution.

I would just smile, thinking of my contribution as a village chief and my previous life as an activist and rebel. And then I am reminded of the Army camp nearby that turns out soldiers with the passion to fight as much as we revolutionaries do.

But the greatest triumph for revolutionaries like me is to see idealism transformed into practical endeavors that truly serve the people.

Juanito Rivera
Founding Group, New People's Army

A Rebellion Within

When I was young, I was always active in church. On Saturdays and Sundays, I was always in our church because I was active in our youth organization in San Lorenzo Ruiz in Davao. Even when I was in high school, I would see the nuns, the shepherd sisters who really help the poor. I guess those images I saw inspired me to be like them, and I even met some of those nuns even after I graduated from college.

After graduation, I met them again and I was vaguely aware of a spark inside me. I was already working at our parish but I felt something was still missing. The nuns told me to try the vocation. I saw how they helped others, like the unwed mothers and the street children. Because I have a soft spot for street children, I was deeply touched by their work.

My 3-year formation was spent in Manila and my desire to serve became even stronger. I really wanted to serve the Lord by helping the poor street children and the unwed and abandoned mothers-to-be. Unfortunately, I was sent to a Northern Mindanao tribal apostolate. I never even knew that such a tribe existed, and that there are people like the *lumads* who also needed help, and I took pity on them, too.

The sisters told me that no one else helped the *lumads* except for us were like gods there, helping them. So I thought, wow, this would really be an accomplishment, if I get to help these people in dire need, especially the children. So I helped by giving school lessons, reading and writing lessons.

I loved the service that we, the nuns, offered to the tribal people.

We also went to the mountainous regions where we saw the malnourished children with big stomachs. We would bathe them in the river, then we would take pictures of them, and their dilapidated houses. I later learned that these pictures accompanied our project proposals to ask for foreign funds. So that was when I understood our advocacy work.

After only six months, I discovered the secret connection with the rebels. I was not surprised because there were a number of priests and nuns who, because of their passionate advocacy, had already aligned themselves with the revolutionaries.

I was always the one left to guard the house and they always left instructions that somebody would pass by to pick up something. Sometimes it was rice, sometimes money. One time, they were picking up a gallon of gasoline, but instead of gasoline, it was full of bullets. That won't be inspected in any military detachment because it will be mistaken for gasoline. They were M16 bullets. I was wondering what the bullets were for. There was also another clueless nun like me, and eventually we discovered the connection. She made the mistake of speaking over our radio one time, saying: "Sister, the rebels who will pick up the rice are already here." She got scolded big-time. As for me, I never said anything aloud but I had lots of questions. "What was that? Why was it like that?"

I followed instructions. And I played a lot of roles in following those orders. Whenever some rebel commander would come down, I would act as their guide and wear my habit. We had a jeep and whenever we would pass a detachment, they would let us go because there was a nun inside. Sometimes I helped by bringing pregnant women in labor. Whenever somebody needed medical attention, I would bring them to Davao. Sometimes, the rebels I would accompany for check-ups would panic whenever they see soldiers. I would tell them to keep calm because I was wearing my veil then I also told them that they should never underestimate its strong power. I wasn't really comfortable wearing the veil but during those times, I was forced to use it because it gave us protection.

My indirect assistance proved to be most helpful. I helped them acquire foreign funds by organizing the youth. I would gather the youth and do projects like tree-planting, conduct symposiums, or support farms, whatever activities were needed. We would tell them and show these activities in our project proposals and we received foreign funding because of these activities.

Yet something was amiss in handling of the funds. I was the

one always tasked to check with the banks if our foreign funding already arrived. I was ordered to withdraw money from our accounts. We would use that to buy rice that would be given to the *lumads* in their communities. But I never saw them receiving much. So I began asking questions in my mind. I saw huge amounts being spent on things I did not know about.

I was wondering where all that money was going. I began questioning this within myself, if those were the values we were supposed to be teaching the youth. We taught them loyalty, trust, honesty. But where was honesty in our own ways and workings? I couldn't share my suspicions with anybody. Whatever our superiors would prohibit us to do, I went ahead and did them, that was my kind of personal rebellion. I didn't know how to handle or cope with that situation so I guess I was also ruining myself by doing that. I had no solid proof and just kept everything to myself.

Right before I married, I served my congregation with a strong sense of purpose. That is me at the center.

I was hanging out a lot with some of the young professionals who were also working with us. Whenever they would ask me to go with them, to have fun, relax by drinking, going out at night, I would go with them. But I didn't know that my behavior reached my mother superior. So of course, as a young sister, I was scolded. I wanted to make a rebuttal and remind her that we are good shepherds, so a good shepherd leaves the 99 in the flock to search for that one wayward and lost sheep. But of course it was useless to argue. I guess because of my frustrations with the sisters, I was driven to find solace in other people, which led me to become close friends with a *lumad* man, until our friendship developed into love. They were really mad at me for having a boyfriend. When they discovered this, they asked me to choose: my boyfriend or the sisterhood. I chose my boyfriend.

Well, at least with the decision I made, I was being honest: I will live honestly and without lies. I was just being true to myself. The man I married was the son of a supreme tribal chief whose entire tribe was sympathetic to the rebels. From what I saw when I first went to my husband's village, they seemed to have been neglected for so long. The government was just too far away — at least 40 kilometers from the remote village. They were also told that the government already abandoned them and that only the rebel organization cared for them. In a way, I believed that, because I saw how the local and national government neglected the *lumads*. They lacked essentials like education and food. The youth did not really know much about anything except for what the rebels teach them. Having seen all these led me to believe that perhaps what the rebels were saying were true all along, and that the government was wrong.

But before I could develop my full sympathy for the rebel cause, I was blacklisted, and left by my congregation on my own. I somehow accepted that because a former nun marrying a tribal man was not good for the congregation's reputation, but I never foresaw the hardships of transitioning from a nun to a married woman.

I was jobless for a few years after that. Our only job then was small-scale logging business, gathering vines and stuff, nothing big. Because of the suspicion that I might squeal on the movement's financial mismanagement secrets, my husband's family was cursed too. While my father-in-law had been a loyal rebel supporter for many years, providing as many tribal fighters as he can muster, he became an outcast after that. He was excluded from meetings and left out of planning sessions.

The years after my marriage to a tribal prince, were the most difficult for me.

The rebels and the other members of the tribe connived against my father-in-law. We were barred from tilling the land, and partaking of whatever economic benefits were derived from the financial aid coming from outside. We were desperate for food and money. We didn't have anybody left to turn to for help or work. Our entire clan, including my father-in-law who was the tribal chief, was eased out by the rebels who resented me.

But I still harbored hopes that somehow, we could patch things up with the rebels, so that we could live in peace, under their supervision and control. I was willing to take that compromise for the sake of my newborn son. But one incident changed my perception of the rebels forever.

That incident really tore me apart, and broke my heart. I met a young girl, a *lumad,* who was very beautiful, intelligent, and fair-skinned. She had a problem with her family and that was what led them to recruit her. She approached me one day and said she will go fulltime with the rebels as she was losing hope, that she saw nothing will change for the better, so she might as well do something. She killed one of the barangay officials in their area as a test for her. I asked her why she had to kill someone innocent, and she said it was what her officials ordered, so she had to obey. One time, she went with a group who went to gather sweet potatoes for their food. Just then, soldiers were going commando style, and were walking around in civilian clothes. One of the soldiers pretended to be one of the rebels, and approached someone to ask if he saw his other "companions." Thinking that the soldier in civilian clothes was actually a rebel, the person pointed him towards the sweet potato plots. And there, the soldiers spotted the group of rebels gathering sweet potatoes.

The soldiers were able to trap them, asked them to surrender, but they fought, and she was killed there. She was just 17 years old then, so young, such a waste. Then the rebels left her body there, and they never claimed her as theirs. Her remains were brought to a funeral home, then the local officials alerted her parents, but her parents didn't want anything to do with her or her corpse. I was just crushed. I began questioning why the rebels wouldn't even help one of their own; that that was what they did to their members. — Even in death, they were abandoned. So we took care of her remains and had them buried. That was really painful for me. All that time I was thinking, if only she had the chance to study, she could have had a bright future, because she was beautiful, intelligent, had good posture and bearing to boot. Such a waste.

But we were getting hungry, and my husband's entire immediate family had nowhere to go. I started blaming myself for the misfortunes of my in-laws. Without me, they could still be enjoying the trust and confidence of the rebels, as much as they have done so for several years. I thought of going back to the congregation again, not as a nun, but just as a plain worker. I just wanted to have my son take a shot at life when times were so hard for me and my husband. But my superiors were hardened. I cried endlessly at what I had done for myself, my husband's family and my child.

My father-in-law, the proud tribal chief that he once was, asked for help from the rebels, who by then had absolute control of his tribe. He just wanted to be assigned a piece of land to till. But the rebels would not allow him. My crime against the organization and to its financial supporters, though I never talked, was just too serious. Anybody who was associated with me was suspect. No one was willing to help us.

In desperation, my father-in-law decided to turn his support to the government side. He was on the order of battle of the military for so long, but this time, he had to do the unthinkable: surrender his tribal clan members. To him, it was the right time to abandon the rebels who, in his dire need would not even help him. He came to believe the government line that the best option was to give up, when the rebels were neglecting us anyway. There were 60 of us -- my husband's relatives, all his siblings, their cousins, other relatives – who came down.

The initial treatment was good, but due to our sheer number, the support from the government was soon depleted. And what made matters worse was that, it took two years before the national government recognized and helped us in earnest. That was a long time, and it even made me think of just going back to the rebels, since the government wasn't giving us enough attention. I was tempted, because I saw that the rebels were are strong as ever. At least they had some money to spend for coffee, they had rice, while we did not.

I signed up with the Philippine Army after my tumultuous past.

It was tempting. But my in-law said no, we gave our word. So finally, after two years, we were given another chance by the military. We were given something for our livelihood. We were given a water buffalo to till our small plots and a motorcycle to haul our agricultural products. These uplifted our lives somewhat. That was when the *lumads* also started having interest in joining as soldiers.

Considering my background, I never imagined I would become a soldier one day. But I signed up and so did my husband. Unfortunately, he died soon after.

Today, I still am in the Army — a former nun, rebel, mother and wife. To be with my family these days, I try my best to go home every Sunday, even just to spend time with them by having breakfast with them, and then I return to camp afterwards. I also tell my children that at least, the dark times are over. Yes, we were together all the time back then, but we had nothing, we were always hungry. At least now, I tell them that they have this chance of going to school, getting an education, having clothes to dress them with, and we have food on the table. So even if I am away from them, it's okay because we could communicate via cellphone anyway, and I also come home whenever I have some free time, even if it's just for an hour.

There is life after darkness. God is merciful.

Corporal Maria Rowena Napongahan
Former rebel nun

A Dose of Our Own Medicine

I do not think the rebellion will ever succeed in the Philippines. But it would not be easy to triumph against it.

But rebels have given up before. I was one of those who abandoned our revolutionary work only because the people rose up against us.

The military is fighting for the hearts and minds of the people. That is what counterinsurgency is all about.

Success lies in the hands of the oppressed, the abused. They are the best purveyors of change, real change.

I am from Agdao, Davao City. I was an organizer in that district in the 80s. Davao City then had 170 communities, one of the largest of which was this semi-industrial district called Agdao. Being a young underground organizer then, I was approached to lead the complete infiltration of the district.

When we started, nobody knew of the New Peoples' Army yet. It was a freewheeling democracy that reigned. Men were drinking in small stores along the narrow streets. The youth were partying everywhere. Children played their games in backyards. Parents did

their best to make a living. I would not say they were totally happy
and free because most of the families were really poor.

We printed a lot of leaflets and newspapers to inform the public of
our plans.

In a matter of months, the atmosphere in Agdao had changed.
We first played heroes by executing petty thieves in front of the
citizens. While they resented the evil deeds of the robbers, the people
were shocked when we paraded their dead bodies for everyone to see.

"We do not tolerate thieves among us," we declared. The public
were just too horrified.

We next went after abusive people in the government. To get
the peoples' support, we told them that government was inherently
good. But some are prone to corruption. The kind of government
we wanted promised a more equal distribution of wealth. Not the
kind where only the rich had power.

"What we do not tolerate are the government people who abuse
their authority," we pointed out. Some have silently shared our
intentions because we all knew that there were a few rotten eggs

serving in government.

We systematically liquidated government people whom we suspected of having a history of bad dealings with the people. Errant policemen were eliminated one by one. One of our assassins would knock on their door as his family was eating dinner. Our assassins pumped bullets into the head and body of our target before his entire family. Our young assassins would be gone, proceeding to another target.

Many of the Agdao citizens left when they could no longer take the violence which local newspapers have already likened to the situation then in Nicaragua. The national media had accurately called Agdao district as "Nicaragdao."

After we drove away those we thought were our enemies, we went into a massive and complete re indoctrination of the people who were left behind. After all, we believed that since they did not leave when everybody else either fled or died, they must be our loyal supporters — or so we thought.

We ran a complete realignment of their values through a rigid re education system — just the way we hoped to when we finally win over the entire country.

"The capitalists use us. The feudal system abuse us, the landlords mistreat us," was our standard line. The people had their own opinions and though theirs were not exactly the same as ours, some of them had the same experiences we described.

Then as if to demonstrate our power, we imposed rules. Lights off at seven, which the people slowly resented because some children were sick and they could not tend to them at night. We also had all the dogs killed because we did not want any barking dog to alert other residents of our presence when we were on the streets. At that time, we had absolute control of the local government. We imposed taxes and tried to learn the art of governance, in case our revolution won.

But all these was short lived as I discovered why the people could only suffer for so long.

They did not like our violent ways. We unwittingly went against traditionally close family ties. Our ways were not appreciated at all. In fact, it soon became clear that we violated their sensibilities.

Led by a barangay captain who asserted his authority as a duly-elected leader, the people began to rise against us.

As the people got tired of our abuses, we were slowly driven into the defensive.

A group called the *'Alsa Masa'* (Rise of the Masses) eventually emerged and went after us.

They hunted me, the political officer and military leader. They reasserted control and killed our most loyal sympathizers, the way we also executed their best leaders a few months before. When we went to seek refuge in a house that we previously thought was safe, we were hunted down by the vigilantes.

The people that we always took for granted rose against us.

Then the people's uprising grew stronger, with a number of people's armed groups joining forces against us. We were vastly outnumbered and beaten by their armed people power.

We ran for our lives, and abdicated control. It was the end of a failed experiment.

I have since given up on the hard life of a revolutionary. I do not think there is hope of the rebellion ever winning. Yet, it remains because it has since become a lucrative underworld business.

I love how Davao City has evolved into a place where people follow the rule of law. But I do not think the city would have such a deep respect for the law had we not taken it into our own hands. We took a dose of our own medicine — and how bitter it was!

Ramon Las Piñas
Rebel political and military officer
in Davao in the 1980's

REBEL STORIES

Just Follow Your Heart

Mine was one of the most stunning defections of a military officer into the rebel side. In the early evening of December 29, 1970, I led a small band of rebels aboard two cars and a military jeep into a lightning raid of a Philippine Military Academy armory. The Superintendent then was out welcoming the President in Baguio City. The cadets were also out for their Christmas break. I was then the officer of the day — in charge of the security of the camp. I had the keys to the armory. Carting away the firearms was a breeze. The 36 rifles, two machineguns and thousands of ammunitions that we carted away from the heart of the nation's premier military school was badly needed by the fledgling rebel movement, established just a year and nine months before that daring action. It was my first mission with the rebel movement I served for the next six long and difficult years.

I was not a typical rebel. My father was a respected member of the tight — knit Army community in Fort Bonifacio. He was the Surgeon General. I idolized him because he brought me into sports — boxing and track and field. I grew up in a Catholic school for boys — La Salle - where we studied the lives of saints. This made a deep impact on my character. My greatest dream as a young man was to become a La Salle brother and have the opportunity to serve the people – just the way the saints have done. But my father prevailed.

"If you want to serve the people, join the military," he advised me. At that time, in the mid 1960's, when I was about to enter the academy as a plebe, massive discontent, street protests and no revolutions were unheard of. But things evolved sharply when the new President stepped in. With his repressive policies, radicalism took root especially among the idealistic students. Even the isolated Philippine Military Academy was not spared.

My special relationship with an ultra nationalistic professor an Academy grad shaped my bold decision to become a rebel. He had a sharp and consistent criticism of imperialism, feudalism and bureaucrat capitalism. Major Cesar Pobre, my professor, was calm and soft-spoken but everybody listened intently. During my last year in the Academy, he invited Jose Maria Sison, who was the head of the *Kabataang Makabayan* (Nationalist Youth) and later became the founder of the Communist Party of the Philippines. He won our young hearts and minds with his patriotic fervor and his strong call – to – action to head to the hills and join his revolution. I signed up against the wishes of my parents. It was against the ideals of the military organization, of which as a cadet, I was already a member of.

Deep in my heart, I wanted to see change in my country. I was thoroughly convinced of another of my Academy professor's arguments that Philippine society was controlled by a few rich families that held most of the wealth. At that time, it was also this group that controlled the government and its instrumentalities, including the Armed Forces. I subscribed to his argument that change cannot happen because this small politically powerful group, the one that also made laws, would exert everything to preserve and protect their economic interests. It was my nationalism that bred my strong motivation to help effect social change. Back then, I had only three options: One was to join a group of other cadets who vowed to stage a *coup d'etat* of sorts after graduation. There were two others who took that option. Both are senators now, but even in their youth, they already believed that they could effect deeper change if they staged popularly supported military uprising that would topple the old order. After a thorough consideration, I realized that it would take more time before it became viable.

For my superior cadet athletic achievements, I got the coveted Athletic Saber Award upon graduation in 1967.

My second option was to join the rebels, who were then mostly students and professors from the University of the Philippines. Because of my strict religious upbringing, I did not fully believe in their godless ideology. I did not really like their Mao Tse Tung inspired — revolution from the countryside strategy that aimed to seize political power through armed struggle. While I was being trained as an officer to be a manager of violence, I felt deep inside that setting effective change through violence was not the right way. I learned this the hard way, but I kept this option open, just in case the third option was to graduate and serve the country as a military man, just the way my highly respected father did. But as fate would have it, my first assignment forced me to seriously consider the rebellion option.

After being trained as Special Forces man and a paratrooper to boot, I got assigned to the constabulary. It may be sad to admit this now, but the abusive individual behavior of this unit drove many moderate reformers to full time radicalized revolutionaries. I felt my values did not harmonize with this constabulary culture. One thing I really disliked was the idea of assigning Academy trained officers as bodyguards of corrupt politicians. Having been shaped under the strict environment of the cadet Honor Code where a cadet was forbidden to lie, cheat, steal or tolerate those who did. Having to secure the personalities who did all these did not sit well with me. I also did not like the politically-motivated missions they gave me. One of those I did not execute was assassinating a mayor. Instead of doing so, I warned him and told him of the plot to kill him. My superiors found out and I became a marked man after that.

Any reservations I had about joining the revolution went away, when I met my future wife. Mely was a very beautiful student. Full of promise, but just like fellow State University students, she was very nationalistic and definitely radicalized. For them, there was an urgent need to take action — with the armed option as the most attractive alternative. After our wedding several months after, Mely and I moved to Baguio City, where I took up a post as Academy instructor. My lectures on social injustice and the unequal distribution of wealth immediately put me under surveillance. Soon after, I met with the rebel leaders. Three weeks after my wife gave birth to our first child, I led the raid on the Academy armory.

My first days and months as a celebrity revolutionary were deeply inspiring. I got assigned to the training department of the then small, communist – inspired rebellion. I loved sharing my military skills to the new recruits. Most of them were from Manila's middle class families. I loved sharing their hardships as well. I used to remind the awe-stricken recruits that we were paid in the Philippine Army to fight. But in the New People's Army, where I took on the *nom de querre* Ka Erning, we did not have salaries, yet we sacrificed for the revolution. Of course, back then, I was unaware that rebel finances were being misspent.

I was part of the inner circle of the revolution. Standing from left: me, Jose Maria Sison, founder of the Communist Party of the Philippines, and Ka Dante, NPA military chief.

I endured the difficulties of the guerilla. Sometimes we would not eat for days. There was a time where government troops were in hot pursuit and we hid for four days without eating anything. There was also a time when all we ate were bananas for eleven days. It was a hard existence. There was even a time when my entire group suffered from diarrhea because we had been eating only coconut meat for days. No matter how rugged life was, I was determined to prove that I chose the right path.

I was sincere in joining the rebellion and training the new rebel recruits.

During those times, I did not mind the accusation that I was a traitor to my father and those that condemned my switching sides. I felt I was following the dictates of my heart, and the principles that I believed in.

I was fighting the very same classmates that I trained at the Academy with.

I also did not mind that my wife was arrested a few months after I defected. She left our three-week old baby to her parents and was promptly whisked away after news of our armory raid broke the news. Her maternal instincts were so strong, she just had to visit our son. This visit led to her arrest.

My desire to rejoin her and our son coincided with my growing disillusionment with revolutionary deception. This started my 'softening' process in the next few years. I longed for family life – a normal life with my wife and child. Yet there I was in the jungle with fellow rebels. I longed for my wife who had inspired me to follow this untrodden path.

But it was the internal corruption within the rebel leadership that made me consider going back to the fold. There was a time when I was assigned to organize a guerilla front in the boundary of Nueva Vizcaya and Nueva Ecija.

Since we did not have a mass base of popular support back then, we could not rely on the villagers to feed us. What made it worse was that, our rebel leadership did not provide funds for our use. We had to rely on the jungle to sustain ourselves. But since we could not survive plainly on bananas and coconuts, I asked for financial support from our leaders. The top rebel military commander came with a few thousand pesos, obviously not enough to sustain us. What made matters worst was that I knew that our top leaders were buying themselves cars and living in air conditioned rooms all from the financial support for the revolution. Yet, there we were surviving in the dense jungle barely eating one full meal every day, unable to buy basic necessities like soap and toothpaste. The underground movement that sought to implement social equality was rotten at its core.

Then came a change of heart. I wanted to go back. I could not handle the deception that was happening around me. I contacted an Academy classmate to facilitate my surrender. I was taken in and immediately placed under maximum security detention together with the fiery oppositionist Benigno Aquino Jr. Like him, I was sentenced by a military tribunal to die by musketry. During those times, I just accepted whatever fate would deal me in the following days. What was most important to me at that point was to be in the loving company of the people that mattered to me most: my wife, my kid and my parents. Our second child was born while both my wife and I were in detention. I was also awaiting execution.

God is good to me and I was eventually pardoned. And to make it even better, I was reinstated as a lieutenant colonel in the Army. With a renewed sense of vigor at this new lease on life, I devoted the following months to writing a book on combating the very same rebels I used to lead. Call me a turncoat, but just like any decision I made in the past, I just followed my heart. To me the sounds of one's heart can be purer than the schemes made up by the mind. Sure, I made unpleasant decisions in the past and may have caused my loved ones severe embarrassment, but I was just being human. I have gone on to do other things, including becoming a one-star general and more surprisingly, head of the Armed Forces intelligence service. Would these turn of events surprise you and me?

At the end of the day, I believe one could truly lead a fuller and definitely, a more colorful life if he just followed his heart.

Major General (retired) Victor Corpus
Former top rebel commander

In The Name Of The Father

The rebel wing that now operates in the Caraballo and Sierra Madre mountains of Nueva Ecija, Nueva Vizcaya and Aurora bears the name of my late husband-Arcadio Peralta. In 1977, in Bongabong, Nueva Ecija, he was a plain farmer, with no intentions of ever joining an armed rebellion. But as fate would have it, one of the survivors of the rebel Long March from Isabela, was his relative. The group of 37 rebel pioneers soon contracted my husband to act as courier and errand boy.

The rebels first became famous by going after the cattle rustlers in our province. After killing the most notorious members of the family that ran the land grabbing and cable rustling operations, the group became instant folk heroes.

Members of the New People's Army had something to say about every issue. They protested the prices of agriculture produce being bought from the farmers at very low prices. Its famed military commander, Ka Dante, had to pose as a legitimate trader to know the real issues first hand. Even the founder of the Party, Joma Sison, set up an office in the town of Talavera to truly understand the workings of the feudal agricultural system that they were trying to destroy.

I became the courier of secret messages between the pioneering top leaders of the New People's Army and the Communist Party of the Philippines.

I brought my first two kids into the world as my late husband was fast making his name as a fiery revolutionary. By the time my eldest, Rick, was in grade one at seven years old and my other child at nine months old, we had been deeply entrenched in the underground movement.

Our first kid was a true son of the revolution.

Whenever students or professors evaded arrest in Manila, they came to me – Nelia Sancho, Horacio Morales all the people who are now immortalized in the annals of the revolution, I met them all. And in one way or another, my husband and I were instrumental in giving them a sanctuary when they needed it most.

My husband became the commander of the rebels in Nueva Ecija in the early 1980's. He soon became known as a ruthless executioner of enemies of the people. My husband, a farmer who had not even finished his elementary education, was the supreme judge of whether a politician, policeman, lived or died. His legend grew until he became so hot and the authorities were so quick on his tail that he was reassigned to an entirely different area. At that time, I was bearing the burden of parenthood alone.

I brought my children to convents that took care of the young children of revolutionaries. With nuns taking care of their kids, rebel leaders were free to roam and do their work.

At that time, I knew we were fast becoming irresponsible parents. When I finally took my children from the convents, my children had begun blaming us for their condition. They were our true children, but my husband and I were the father and mother of the revolution in Nueva Ecija. The revolution at that time, occupied most of our attention.

My husband died in a lightning raid executed by an Army unit soon thereafter. This was an inglorious death, but his name was soon immortalized by being carried as the official name the revolutionary command that he started.

At first I did not know what to do, whether to carry on the revolution or stop my involvement altogether. There was something in me that said I should keep the flame alive. There was also this tiny voice that told that I was already tired. But because the name of my husband at that time, elicited awe, I had to keep inspiring the next generation of rebel recruits.

True enough, one of my sons Rick dared to follow his father's footsteps. He did not seem to mind that he could also die as violently as his father did. He did not seem, to mind that he had a legacy to uphold. He was his own person, because he really grew up without us, without the loving affection of parents.

Just like his father, he shot up like a star as a young rebel commander. Born into a famous revolutionary family, he had a respectable pedigree that others were not as fortunate to have.

Factions developed within the underground movement which severely weakened it.

But his path was to be strewn with controversies. Factions eventually formed between the traditionalists and the reformists. In the bitter turf war as to which side should dominate, my son found himself in one group. Naturally, there was an adverse reaction in the opposing group. Both masters at propaganda, the erstwhile unified rebel army was divided and in bitter tussle against each other. My son was unjustly portrayed as a crook, a mass murderer, a hired gun, a mercenary and all other accusations designed to destroy him.

I really protested because he was a son of the revolution. He grew up in a convent because, we his parents, did not have time for him. He joined the rebellion on his own.

Yet the infighting continued. He was soon portrayed as the leader of the holdup gang that preyed on businesses in Nueva Ecija. This pained me because my late husband, his father, really lived the teachings of the rebellion – do not steal from the masses. He was a role model to them.

The heavy infighting led to serious accussations being hurled at
rival factions.

At one time, I angrily demanded the other group to remove the name of my husband from the history of the countryside revolution. I told them that if they continued to persecute our son that way, they might as well forget all our contributions to the growth of the rebellion in my province.

My son was soon captured and incarcerated. My eyes were heavy with tears as I visited him behind bars.

"Is that what the revolution gives us in return for decades of faithful service?" I murmured to myself.

My son was not repentant, and neither was I. Deep in my heart we did not commit anything to tarnish the name of his father.

Yet, I thought to myself that had we not gotten involved in the rebellion in the first place, we would just be normal citizens going on with our daily lives. Now, we were paying for the decisions that we made. Up to now, I still cannot say if I did the right thing when I joined the revolution, or if my son was also right in following our footsteps.

I just hope that my son's son, my grandson, would make a better decision than we did when he finally chooses his life's direction.

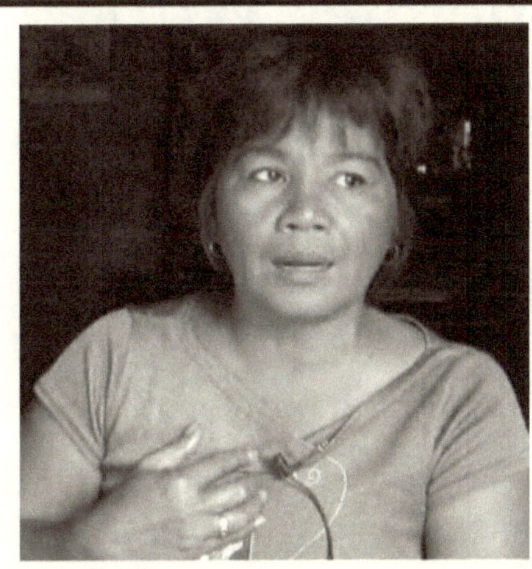

Norma Peralta
Rebel pioneer in 1975

When Former Enemies Work Together

I am old now. I am already in my early 70's. And in my lifetime, I have seen the evolution of the revolution. In fact, I was one of the earliest participants in what has become a series of Muslim Mindanao separatist movements.

I started out as a volunteer for the Muslim vigilante group called the Blackshirts. In the late 1960's, the band of Christian vigilantes called the *Ilagas* had rampaged many of our villages. Led by the legendary Commander Toothpick, who was reputed to have a powerful set of talismans, these bands proclaimed that they were just defending their lands. They were settlers and they guarded their newly acquired lands fiercely. In the absence of a strong and credible Army presence back then, we felt the need to organize our own vigilante group - the Blackshirts. Our uniform was black and our methods to fight our enemies were also black.

There was no widespread war then. Our skirmishes with our rival vigilantes were few and far between. In fact, Mindanao was peaceful back then.

But the issues grew to explosive proportions when the former President declared Martial Law and sent constabulary men and soldiers to Mindanao. That was when things blew up. I do not know who really started the downward spiral - was it the fiery MNLF founder who rallied us against the dictator in Manila whom they said was out to annihilate all Muslims? Or was it the Armed Forces, exaggerating whatever power they wielded — to the point of abuse?

We fought the soldiers implementing Martial Law in the early 1970's.

At that time, I was already a strike force commander in charge of three remote Muslim - dominated municipalities. We resented and retaliated against the heavy handed tactics of the military. The early conscripts then, so different from the soldiers now, were literally drafted from the farms in Luzon. A military truck would park in a village, and require all able-bodied men to go and fight with the Army in Mindanao. Most of those who went on as military draftees were the undereducated farm boys who never heard of cultural and religious rights. And with their newfound power as Martial Law implementors in Mindanao, they were as ferocious as they could get.

We reacted, retaliated, fought and the war just escalated. The effect of Martial Law polarized Muslims and Christians. It was chaotic. The Martial Law implementors, followed no law. Anything they felt they could and want to do, they just did. Things got even worse when foreign governments took sides and supported us. I was, in fact, one of the first 300 fighters sent to Libya to train in guerrilla tactics. With our solidarity with brother Muslims from all over the world, we came back to the Philippines more inspired to wage our holy war. Back then, the whole revolution had been transformed from settling land problems to a religious war, which made us angrier.

I witnessed the heaviest fighting in the following years. I also saw entire families die. I have seen villages burn. I have been witness to violence and hatred between brother Filipinos. The fighting even came to insane proportions where hatred, not reason had become the norm.

We were hopeful of peace when we broke bread with the Armed Forces of the Philippines.

But warriors get tired and when they rest, they dream of peace. I was enlightened about the futility of war when we started talking among ourselves, the original revolutionaries, about the possibilities of going for the unthinkable — initiating a peace agreement with the Philippine government, that up until then, we despised. In a gesture of faith in building peace once more, we signed an agreement in 1976, a few years after the war had claimed thousands of lives on both sides. This first, tentative step towards lasting peace was not implemented to the letter, at least as far as we were concerned. We grew frustrated at the slow pace of its implementation. Since then, some became rebels once more. One of our younger leaders, in fact, organized a breakaway entity out of exasperation. He felt as hopeless as many others and doubted the sincerity of the government to completely honor the agreement.

We embraced the peace and reconciliation program offered by the new President Fidel V. Ramos, a former general.

But I kept the faith and believed in the basic goodness of the agreement, no matter how impractical and possibly flawed its provisions could be. I must admit, there were also times when I felt the peace process was as hopeless. But every time, I picked myself up and started re reading provisions and the principles from which these were derived. Years passed until another government, this time under President Fidel Ramos, once more offered the hand of peace. We again believed him and much to our surprise, things turned out to be better. Much of it really came from the goodwill of enlisting our former fighters into the Armed Forces and the Philippine National Police. Finally, our seasoned fighters could put their skills into use, this time for the government that truly and legally represented them. Many of us also welcomed the livelihood development packages that were part of the reintegration program. Having seen the worst of war, many of us took the opportunity to rebuild our shattered family lives.

But I loved the role that was eventually given to me. As a senior member of our rebel group, I was assigned to be one of the representatives in talks with the government. Among those that I immediately befriended was a senior colonel who was so delighted with the possibility of peace. So, unlike those whom I have dealt with before, this military officer did not have the heavy baggage of war. I immediately liked him as a brother. That, to me, was the turning point of my revolutionary career. After decades of fighting government troops, I finally trusted one of them again.

He eventually got assigned as an Army brigade commander in my area after a few years. And as both people on the ground this time, we went into full gear to sincerely implement the peace agreement provisions.

We built schools together in areas that had the heaviest animosity against the military for the longest time. We distributed medicines donated by the non government organizations. We worked hand in hand, brother to brother, not only to win peace but to sustain it, once and for all.

But what was dramatic about the gestures of my senior military friends, who have grown in number through the years, is the respect they give us in consulting us, their senior former enemies about possible government peace policies. After all, it is us, those who have seen the ugly face of war, that know these best.

Today, I enjoy my special advisory relationship with the military peace advocates. It is really about time that we listen to each other again.

Faisal Karudin
Former senior Moro rebel commander

Double Standard

Mine was probably the best job that a rebel could get: I collected revolutionary taxes. I was born and raised in the city, and the underground movement had a special need for one who could ride a motorcycle, who can type on "official" rebel stationery, who knows how to withdraw from banks and who knew his way around the large cities. Most of my lesser educated rebel comrades do not have these requirements. I breezed through the test!

We were first given a typewriter and freshly printed stationery. Then we got our first tour of our job through a more experienced cadre from another province.

"On that stationery, you must be very professional about the intention of the movement," he started.

"It must never come out as an extortion letter, but rather as a demand for security services we render his business," he continued. I could not believe my ears because I could never imagine charging so much for the mere threat that we would do damage if he did not pay up.

"Always put your letters in nice envelopes, and never send these without your signatures," he finalized his instructions.

That was so awesome! We were in business!

We first went to a gas station. That was the easiest to transact with. We did not have to say that with a single match stick, we could set the multimillion peso investment on fire.

While our comrades in the mountains could hardly get by, we enjoyed life collecting revolutionary taxes in the cities.

"How much did you say you wanted per month?" inquired the owner. When we stated the figure, he immediately knew what to do. He would just pass it on as additional gasoline price to the consumers. That was so easy, so illegal and definitely so unfair for that legitimate businessman.

With each collection, we first bought food, some clothes and cigarettes before we remitted any amount we collected. Compared to our buddies in the mountains who could barely sustain their cigarette needs without any allowance, we lived large. We bought the more expensive brand rather than the local brand that our comrades had to make do with.

We then went to the trucking and bus companies. Their fleet of vehicles plied the highways from town to town. The owners knew the dangers. We would just hail one of their buses, bring down all the passengers, and burn the bus in some isolated portion of the highway. Many trucks and buses had been torched because their owners were uncooperative.

"How did you want me to bring me the money," asked the decently-dressed entrepreneur.

Our guerillas in the mountains had to ask from poor rural folk for food and other needs.

"You could deposit through our ATM account or you can have one of your representatives deliver it to us," we gave our instructions. Our activities were done in the name of the revolution. That it was normal practice. Every businessperson seemed to just regard the amounts they gave us as cost of doing business. We were happy.

But our commanders were happier. While our comrades slept on rags and rugged tents deep in the mountains, the leaders of the movement had big houses in subdivisions. They had cars, servants, and they sent their children to expensive private schools. We knew but the fighters never did. But we were not complaining. We were having a good time using our power to demand regular taxation from businesses. In fact, we beat the government because no one dared cross our paths.

A contractor of an international airport in Bicol in 2009 dared to challenge us. Apparently, he felt that the 8% of the total project cost we were demanding was too much. He was, in a way, correct because we were really demanding the moon. His option was to absorb our imposition and pass it on in the form of lesser quality and unsafe runway or airport facilities and risk losing his AAA contractor's license. Or he would refuse to pay us and risk the damages we can bring to his business. When he chose the latter, we attacked him — burned his bulldozers, loaders and all other essential equipment needed to complete the project. He must have learned from that bitter lesson, as much as a few more enlightened contractors had. We simply had to have a cut in all projects.

We eventually saw the lifestyle of our city-based leaders. One appeared so legitimate that he was even elected parent-teacher association president of the exclusive elementary school of his children. Meanwhile, we also knew how miserable our comrades were in the mountains. Their underwear were already ripped apart, their slippers had holes and their shirts, tattered.

"Where does all the money that we collect go to anyway?" I had to ask myself, even if the answer was obvious.

Our more lucrative source of income was the permit to campaign fees we demanded from each election candidate. For the more unscrupulous ones, they simply offered large sums in the millions or hundreds of thousands without being asked. I never found out how much we asked from candidates for national offices. But I had seen candidates for governor pay within the range of two to five million each. For mayoralty candidates, the permit to campaign fee was at least three hundred thousand each. I really could not understand why they even had to pay us when we really did not totally control any territory. Maybe because we were perceived as having such power that we could just use it against them. We amassed so much money from elections that no one could imagine how it was all spent.

The fighters in the mountains never really knew the large amounts we were collecting in the cities.

Yet the people that carried the rifles, those upon whose firearms our real power came from, those who offered their lives for the revolution, did not receive as much. I knew it because in several instances, our poor fighters would swap their worn out clothes with the newer ones we were wearing every time we went up and met them in their hideouts. They clearly, were not benefitting from the money that we had been collecting.

I thought about this for a long time. And I thought, such hypocrisy! We all professed to join because we wanted to institute changes in society, we wanted a more equal distribution of wealth, yet those whose very lives were at stake received the least! We had been so corrupted even before we would even win. The more I thought about it, the more I believed that winning was not necessary as all we needed to do was to sustain what has become an extortion racket.

Why do we have to surrender when we are making money as rebels?

I gave up after a few years of doing my work. Someone took over real fast!

Ka Borris
Former revolutionary tax collector
in Bicol

A Birth Triumphs Over Grief

I grew up without a father. I remember my mother telling me as a kid that my father was already in Heaven, among the angels. I believed her until I discovered how he died.

My mother kept secrets but the worst she had kept, she told me right after I graduated from elementary school.

"I was four months pregnant with you then," she tearfully narrated.

"They came barging into our house, all armed men. I knew they were rebels," she declared. I was crying when she recounted the story.

"I never heard from him afterwards," she continued.

"They say he was buried somewhere, but I never found his body," my mother sobbed.

From then on, and throughout four years of high school, the idea of knowing the circumstances of my father's death consumed me. I felt I would never be complete as long as the question remained unanswered.

I was seventeen years old, and already in my first year of college when a rebel recruiter approached me.

"Do you want to know why your father was killed, who killed him and where his body is buried?" he temptingly asked me.

I wanted to know the truth about my father's death. That is why I wanted to become a rebel myself.

"I know the answers," he promised me. I soon was persuaded to join them. Just like many impressionable young people, it was not actually their ideology nor the changes they wanted to make that attracted me.

I was eighteen when I became a fulltime rebel in Quezon. My first job was to teach the other recruits about society, revolution, ideology and politics. My leaders felt I was too naive asking hard questions. I asked why we had to collect fees and issue permits to campaign and exhort people to vote for those who paid. The candidates wanted to win the elections, but just like businessmen, they did not want to pay us. After all, we were not really doing them any service. We threatened to burn, kill or destroy those who did not pay the taxes we imposed.

I felt that my leaders knew that they would enjoy my support and service as long as they withheld the information I sought.

My commanders withheld all the information I needed until one unintentionally spilled it out.

One of the senior leaders unintentionally told me what I long wanted to hear.

"We killed your father," he confessed.

"Your father was mistaken for a deep penetration agent of the military," he added. I could not believe what he was telling me.

"All his brothers were soldiers, that's why," he concluded. My eyes welled with tears as he recounted the gruesome execution of my father. I cried until my eyes were dry.

It was good my boyfriend from the movement was there during my most painful moment. In my desperation and longing for companionship, I soon married my boyfriend, who just like me, was also a young college kid recruited into the revolution.

I soon married a fellow rebel with whom I could share my innermost thoughts.

Since I already discovered the information I wanted to know, I decided to stay on for the love of my husband, who was bent on making a career as a revolutionary. We belonged to separate groups and we only met each other every four months or so. These were the times when our groups joined to run tactical offensives against the military.

In one instance, I really detested the treatment I got when my husband was not there. Our group was tracked by the military patrol as we negotiated our way through the jungle. At the first burst of fire, two of our comrades lay dead. The fighting was so intense and our commander was so confused, that he ordered an immediate retreat. I did not follow his instructions. I was left behind, in shock. As I made my way out of that kill zone, I was crying. I was crying because I feared the military might capture me, and rape and torture me the way we have always been taught. I was also crying because my comrades left me when I needed them most. I escaped from that place and when I reunited with my troops, I kept silent. I was a changed woman after that. My suspicion that everybody was dispensable was proven right. I kept silent.

Our leaders were not always the most tactically proficient.

I walked out of the rebellion for good on the day that I gave birth to my baby. I was kept in our secret mountain camp for the long months of my pregnancy. But as my delivery day approached, I just wanted to share that joyous moment with my mother who was welcoming her first grandchild into the world. But my leaders would not let me out. By then, they must have been suspicious of my motives of questioning their decisions. And perhaps as a test of my faith, my commander allowed me to leave camp as my labor pains began. It was cruel, but I was desperate, so I walked away knowing that any moment I could give birth. I walked carefully on the side of the road, making sure that if I give birth, at least it will be on the healthy bed of grass by the road. I was crying because I felt my womanhood was violated and trampled upon by my commander.

I was bearing the pain of labor as I walked into the nearest village by myself. I must have walked for at least three hours, when I felt that my baby was about to come out. I could already see the nearest house, and by my estimate, it was just about five minutes away. But my baby had to come out.

I delivered my baby on that grassy side of the road, all by myself, in that lonely mountain in Quezon. As my baby cried for the first time, I cried too. I was finally free.

Marife Abraham Benosa
Former rebel in Quezon

Rebels in Paradise

I never imagined that Bohol would turn out this way. Up until a massive earthquake hit this beautiful province in 2013, it was the center of tourism in the Philippines. Its crystal blue waters and beautiful beaches with pristine white sand beckoned tourists weary of city life. The dive sites featured biodiversity that was a thrilling attraction to explorers. And those unique, boat serenades that treated tourists to song and dance numbers as they cruised through the palm tree-lined, green river was definitely a memorable experience. For several years now, the island province was peaceful on Sundays. You could see the pious citizens go to church together, ever religious, as they had always been. Businesses were sprouting left and right as foreigners sought hotels and resorts. It was so common to see fair skinned tourists going for adventure bike rides to explore the caves, rivers and other attractions.

But Bohol was not always this peaceful. In fact, it was referred to as the poor, conflict — stricken province for almost two decades until development and peace came together.

I feel that I am partly to blame for the violent reputation of Bohol. I started the armed struggle there in 1981. With just three followers and the permission of the revolutionary party, we disengaged from our operations in nearby Surigao and set out to exploit the poverty of the island province of Bohol. Revolution was not new to the people. In fact, the central part of the province, which has an amazing labyrinth of caves and natural tunnels, was the sanctuary of the famous Dagohoy, who has the record of leading the longest revolt against the Spaniards just a century earlier.

Nobody has heard of the New Peoples' Army when our team landed in Bohol in 1981.

My small group did not have a single firearm when we landed in the province. We just had machetes to use in case somebody attacked us. The authorities then did not ever suspect that a small group of unnamed persons led by me were trying to foment armed rebellion. We were free to roam. We agitated the masses. Poverty was the easiest to exploit. When a poor man who had barely enough food to put on the table heard of our plans to turn everything around so that he can feed his family three square meals a day, he joined. Whenever I talked about having experienced injustice which made me join the rebellion after having been unjustly incarcerated for a crime I was eventually found innocent of, a number agreed and joined me. When I told them about how we tamed the infamous lost command of vigilantes who abused people at will in Surigao, they found the strength to fight together. They did not really feel the urgent need to revolt because the authorities back in 1981 were not as fierce and greedy as the Spanish *conquistadors*. But we were so adamant about their need to fight, that by the first year we had 300 supporters with seven firearms. Compared to the other areas like Davao, which already faced an insurgency situation by then, our small accomplishment was nothing. We had a long way to go and my 'legend' had just begun. My record of success in the areas where I was ordered to organize the supporters and the armed groups was beyond compare.

We shot into national prominence when we shocked the Philippines with our lighting raid on a police station inside a municipal hall in the sleepy inland town of Batuan. We closely observed the behavior patterns of the policemen guarding the police station. They were alert at night, but on Sunday mornings, religious as they all were, they abandoned the station to go to church with their families. We exploited this weakness and raided the station on a Sunday morning. We took with us all their firearms. News that the peaceful province of Bohol was aflame with rebellion spread far and wide after that.

I was determined to make a name. We followed with another raid at a police station. It was a classic one that we pulled off. We brought police uniforms and borrowed a jeep that we also painted with police markings. Our plan was to disguise ourselves as policemen and just like in the movies, raid a police station. To make things authentic, we even had our hair cut just the way the law enforcers wore their hair: short. The bewildered policemen were incredulous when we arrived.

"There is no order to inspect our firearms," remarked the police chief.

"Yes, there is. There is the written order," I showed a fake police readiness inspection order.

"Gather all your firearms here, so we could inspect them one by one," I ordered the suspicious chief. He reluctantly ordered the armory open and had their firearms laid out as neatly as possible.

Then out of the blue, my other people pointed their guns at the policemen who were already aligned to be inspected. They could not believe their eyes, when we introduced ourselves as rebels. They were tricked. It seemed like a scene straight out of a comedy movie.

We pulled so many more of those daring raids and ambushes that by the late 1980's, Bohol was on fire. Scout Rangers soon tracked us down. I suffered casualties within my ranks, which had numbered in the hundreds by then. Yet we persevered and continued to fight. My transformation did not come from soldiers' bullets. Mine came from the rottenness of the revolutionary movement that I was loyal to for 25 years.

While I joined the revolution because I perceived a rotten system of justice, I never imagined that the organization that posed as the alternative was even more despicable. Much of it really came from financial abuse of the revolutionary taxes they amassed. They promised me and the people whom I convinced to join, that our lives would get better. They pledged their lives for that dream. But nothing happened. In fact, their families were poorer because the fathers who could have been breadwinners, were out hiding in the mountains, chasing an empty dream.

But one thing that really made me a marked man was when our leaders could not accept the harsh criticism I posed when they ordered us to rob banks. I would understand that one moment when in our first year of setting up the insurgency, I complied with the order. We simply were without any money to run our operations. Even if I know that it was not government money but people's hard-earned deposits that we were stealing. I justified my actions as something necessary for the revolution. But to continue to order us and other groups in neighboring Cebu to rob banks was not only criminal, it was so totally against our principles.

Despite all the sacrifice for the revolution, ordinary fighters never received the support their families were promised.

I have since given up, and have become a vocal critic of the rebellion. Over the radio, I keep trying to convince my comrades to all come back to the fold. Many have followed my example. In fact, we had been instrumental in the rehabilitation of Bohol.

We were responsible for having started the conflict. Our group must now also help the government regain the peace that once reigned before my band of agitators set foot in Bohol in 1981.

Knowing that I had seen the full cycle of the rebellion and

having witnessed the rapid economic development because Bohol is peaceful once more, I feel that it is my responsibility to continue to help keep it safe.

Revolutionaries do not all die young. Some, like me, live to see a beautiful story unfold.

Epitacio Ramirez
Organizer of Bohol rebellion
in 1981

Life is Precious

I cannot forget the firefight against the Philippine Marines on that day in Zamboanga del Norte in 1986. It started at 6:30 in the morning, and as noon approached, there was no sign of let up. We were running out of bullets and rocket propelled grenades. A few more hours, and we would have been overrun. Three of my men were dead and seven, severely wounded. We were only 50 meters apart and we knew the Marines had casualties too. We spotted several of their casualties lying on the ground. They couldn't pick those up because of the heavy fighting. The clash ended at around 8 pm when it was already too dark to fire.

As we recovered our dead the following day, we also found casualties from the Philippine Marine Corps. As we picked up our dead, I ordered my men to respect those of the Marines. Back then, it was unheard of for us to leave the bodies of our enemies alone. It was common practice to mutilate the corpses to prevent their souls from entering heaven.

We buried our dead with the traditional rituals befitting slain *mujahideen*. It occurred to me that protracted fighting rendered lives utterly worthless!

"Do not bury the others," I told my men. I knew that they would search for them. I wanted them to be found and brought back to their waiting families.

We, the Tausugs, have a fierce fighting tradition.

Both sides lost lives for this revolution. For the soldiers who swore to defend the Philippine Constitution from enemies like us, they professed to be ready to die for their country. I do not think their families were as ready. For most of the Marines, service to the country was also their means of livelihood, their source of income. When they died, their families would get a modest pension. It was highly unlikely that their sons would follow in their footsteps.

But for our dead martyrs, it was an entirely different story. When one of us died, his bereaved family did not receive anything. He will leave his family as poor as they had been — no future, no income no prospects. Except if the son decided to take up arms, to follow his dead father's path. Along with other boys whose fathers died, they would take up arms too. With angry hearts, their vengeful spirits would be the fresh, young blood that would feed the revolution.

I am a second generation fighter. I was still a small kid when the fighting raged in my town of Basilan in the early 1970's. But I grew up hearing the sounds of angry gunfire, of crying widows, and of fatherless children. After all, I am from one of the fiercest ethnic groups in the region.

My clan members had been fighting for generations.

The original Abu Sayyaf terrorists were sons of Basilan — and most of them were from my hometown. They were the "new kids on the block" whose tactics were similar to ours. But our motivations were different. They fought for a separate Moro land, separate from the Philippine Republic. These young ones seemed to have succumbed to the lure of ransom money they got from kidnapping. They preyed on tourists, businessmen and personalities who could pay them what they demanded. Some paid the ransom because they could afford it. Those who could not, ended up dead — decapitated, raped, mutilated. The business was booming at the expense of the country's image and the lives of those involved — especially the soldiers.

I watched how they grew from a small group of religious fanatics to an unruly band of terrorists. Through the years, many more joined them because they took care of the communities they called their camps and sanctuaries. When everybody benefitted from the ransom money, it became a business. I grew up in the ideals and dreams of separatism. I witnessed the transformation of that dream in the hands of the bandits who took advantage of the poverty of their supporters.

I was picked as one of the former rebel commanders who were integrated into the Armed Forces of the Philippines as an officer. I did not imagine I would have a regular salary as an officer. The income was something that eluded me throughout my years as revolutionary. Somehow, it was a positive thing for me.

Yet there were also risks and mine seemed greater than my fellow soldiers, as my first assignment was in Basilan, my home province. For fear of rebel reprisals against family members left behind, soldiers were seldom assigned to their hometown. Yet, on my first day, I was ordered to pack my bags to augment the troops already engaged in another combat operation.

I knew it was going to be complicated. I was manning the mortar, and if one of the terrorists spotted me, he would think I had become a traitor to the tribe. I dreaded the possibility that my family would fall victim to reprisals. I did my duty, fired those mortar rounds even if I knew I was once one of them. The fighting stopped on the third day, and we began collecting the bodies of the casualties.

With my relatives residing in Basilan, it was very hard to go back and fight against them.

Memories rushed back when we picked up a slain Abu Sayyaf. Unlike the other casualties that were successfully extricated by their comrades, this young one was left alone, behind a coconut where he sought cover until one bullet killed him. Just like the Marine we discovered and later left in the battlefield to be picked up by his buddies, this one had to be given respect too.

"Give him the proper ceremony and let us leave his body to be picked up by his family," I ordered. Then all the memories of my past, most of which I do not wish to relive, came back again.

In the battlefields of Mindanao, the lives of combatants can be cheap. They are wasted unnecessarily sometimes, for a cause, or sometimes selfish interests. I pity the families who will have to bear such losses.

Today, my Army commanders respect my desire to safeguard

my family from revenge if I engage in combat operations against my terrorist acquaintances. My superiors have assigned to me jobs that I thoroughly enjoy going around my town and province to convince my former comrades and their young sons to consider peace this time. I have seen positive results and that fulfills me now.

Captain Alonto Maamo
Former Moro rebel leader

Accidental Rebel

I was born into a military family. My grandfather, a guerilla in World War II, survived the harrowing experiences of war. He lived with us until he died when I was six years old. In his last years, he talked about the joys of service as a guerilla. Most of his fellow citizens played it safe, some became Japanese collaborators while others simply kept quiet. But my grandfather wanted to do more so he fled to the mountains, attacking Japanese outposts whenever could. The fulfillment and sense of accomplishment of having served his fellow men impressed me, even at that age.

My paternal grandfather was not as fortunate. He too, was a guerilla who reported to an American officer. They were in Corregidor, a fortress island which was eventually given up because of the endless bombings of the Japanese. They were then herded to Bataan and were forced to walk a 130-kilometer march to Tarlac now known as the Death March. He died of starvation and dehydration along with thousands of captured American and Filipino soldiers. We never found his grave.

My father also chose to become an Army officer. He was no ordinary soldier. He sat such a high standard for himself. He took his oath of professionalism seriously. We knew, because despite our family's financial difficulties, he remained clean and always valued integrity. As if conditioning us for the service, my father would take us to military command conferences by public transport, while his fellow officers drove nice cars. He was a senior colonel, yet he took pride in reminding us, his children that if we wanted to be rich, the military was not the profession to be in. He after said that one joined the military to earn respect for the family, not to be rich.

My father followed in the footsteps of his father.

My siblings took his advice to heart. But they were more practical than my father. Two eventually became doctors and one became a lawyer. I chose to follow my father's path, even if it meant keeping his vow of poverty for the sake of honest service.

I could have availed of opportunities to private schools, yet he and my mother, a school teacher, had us attend elementary and high school in the rural public schools where we lived. We could not afford the other things beyond the basic necessities that their combined salaries could afford. But, we all felt the deep respect that our neighbors had for him. This desire to be respected for my professionalism inspired me to seek admission to the Philippine Military Academy and eventually with the Scout Rangers.

I believed back then, as I do now, that one's dedication to the test of professionalism is not credible unless he endures the physical, emotional and psychological challenges of his line of work. Choosing to be with the Rangers meant a very strict commitment to the life of "cutting edge" jungle fighters. This meant living the lives of guerilla hunters and sticking to the demands of this specialized profession. I thoroughly enjoyed the camaraderie among the Rangers.

Ours was a brotherhood that relied on each other regardless of the circumstances. That is me, second from left.

As a fresh recruit into the Rangers, I tried my absolute best to belong. I perfected the one skill every jungle warrior worth his salt had to be the best in — marksmanship. I displayed my proficiency with the rifle when I shot tight shots from as far as 250 meters away with utmost ease. I was eventually picked to join the Army rifle team that competed in several national and international competitions. I did not mind the thousands of hours of practice – dry shooting rifle drills – because I appreciated the value of these to hardening my commitment to my calling. The first real indicator that I truly belonged was when I got tapped to organize the first sniper training in the Philippine Army. Back then, in the mid 1990's secessionists were claiming sovereignty over their camps and territories. With their blatant display of firepower, fierce fire and maneuver tactics, they had registered heavy casualties on government forces over a series of daring firefights. A unit of highly trained killers that could deliver accurate fire from afar was needed.

I formed this group of skilled marksmen in my image. I thoroughly indoctrinated them about being dedicated and committed to their deadly craft. I trained them to endure the hardship that might come their way in their profession.

Deployed for the first few times, my small groups of snipers were tasked to augment mechanized infantry personnel in Maguindanao in 1997. Several of the infantry soldiers had been wounded and had to be evacuated out of the kill zone. My group had to act and save them. I buddied up with a fellow sniper and rushed towards the position of the casualties. But as we picked up our next victim to safety, I got hit. When a bullet shatters your body – any part of it – your dreams suddenly fall apart. I got hit on the neck, and while I was still conscious, I remember thinking that it could be fatal so I had to be evacuated fast. Luckily, one of the pilots supporting us dared to pick us up, despite intense fire. Without his daring deed, I would have died in the battlefield.

My mother thought I was already dead. My sister, who was a

doctor was informed by one of her fellow military doctors that I was already dead - hit on the face and impossible to keep alive. My hysterical mother, the hardened military wife that she was, immediately organized a mass to pray for my soul. She got the surprise of her life when I was airlifted out of that ill-equipped field hospital to the AFP General Hospital where my sister served as a doctor. Despite my bloated face, my devoted wife and my children were very happy to see me. After four months of hospital confinement, I was issued a clean bill of health. I was again fit for military duty. I survived the first unwelcome test of my military professionalism — being wounded in combat.

I was a highly motivated officer who preferred field assignments.

I hardly stepped out of the hospital when I got my orders to be transferred to another troubled spot — Basilan. By then, my wife, whom I married right after graduation, had learned to be as tough as myself. She knew that I derived my strength from my family and the worst that she can do was to drag me out of my service. She had learned not to complain. But on some occasions, she and I cried together. In my long years in the battlefield, we were occasionally given a 15 – day break. I really looked forward to this rest and recreation because I was in Basilan for as long as I could remember. Upon getting the order, I packed my bags, bought some presents for my kids and flew home. I had barely gotten out of my car when the phone rang.

"Gani, can you come back?" Asked my commander on the other end of the line. I did not even think, much more question his order.

"Yes sir. I will just eat sir," I replied.

"Something bad happened in Sulu, and I want you to be there in 48 hours," ordered my commander over the phone.

I spent more time in the company of my soldiers than with my family.

It was the first time that my wife, my kids and I cried together. We were all looking forward to spending time together after a long time of separation. But duty called again, and I responded as a true professional soldier, I waited until my children were asleep before I left so I would not hear them cry. As I stepped out of our humble house, my wife and I cried, not out of sadness, but because we were celebrating my commitment to this demanding profession.

It was this natural feeling to preserve the professionalism of the Armed Forces that drove me a few years after to become a military rebel. When I was assigned to headquarters after 10 continuous years in the battlefield, I got to see how things in our supposedly service – oriented organization were like. A consensus slowly formed among the officers corps of the Scout Rangers that what was happening was far from what a professional military organization must be. We did not want to stay blind and silent about out observations. We first informed our superiors about our issues and concerns. Disappointed over their lack of attention and the slow action on our proposed changes, we decided to act. We wanted to stage a peaceful demonstration of our power to coincide with the Edsa People Power Revolution celebration as detainees. We were all professional and even highly decorated officers. As I contemplated inside my cell, I tried very hard to understand my reality; it was distressing to even come to terms the events that got me into that dirty cell.

Meanwhile my family started disintegrating. My wife of over two decades was unable to handle the pressure of my incarceration for a rebellious act. She attempted to take her life, but was luckily saved by my eldest daughter from doing so. Needing a father figure that my absence could not provide, my children tried to come to grips with our situation. My youngest began cutting classes, and had began to rely more on friends for support. All I could do was cry silently. They were not what I had hoped for my family.

Finding us innocent of the act of rebellion after three years of detention, the military court martial released us. Free at last, I tried very hard to regain lost time with family. It remains a battle to keep our family as tight as I dreamed it to be. It is even harder to come to terms with redefining my self-worth and professionalism. I looked back to the stories of my grandfather and father and how their adherence to the military code of conduct had led them to succeed and earned them respect as well. I believe I still command the admiration and respect of those that I served with. I am back in the groove of military men after the President pardoned us. My fellow "activists and rebels" and I are now below our classmates in the lineal list for promotion. Perhaps we should have exercised restraint, thought things over before we acted on our frustrations. Maybe we should have thought of other ways of airing our concerns. My ideals remain intact, but I have grown wiser as I continue to pay the price for my actions.

Major Isagani Criste
Scout Sniper course organizer

No Small Contribution

I first met the late Father Conrado Balweg when I was thirteen years old. He had just joined the outlawed New People's Army then. His was the first truly sensational story of a priest turning his back against his vocation to join the revolution. He was forced to go underground when the government began to pursue him and others protesting operations that would endanger tribal territory in Abra.

We were mostly highland revolutionaries in my village. We welcomed him with open arms especially because as a new rebel, he did not have blood on his hands yet. We were extremely proud of him because he was the first from the fierce Tingguian highlander tribe to become a priest. More importantly, we saw in him the figure of a liberator - someone who could rally us, the poor and discriminated tribal people into gaining the respect of other ethnic groups. Having proven his devotion to practical social work by serving the parish of a far flung area, we felt that it would not take long for him to help us break away from the bias against highlanders.

The whole Cordillera region was united against the construction of a dam that would flood villages and traditional burial grounds.

To us, we would rather die than to see the remains of our ancestors desecrated. For us, there was no other choice but to arm ourselves. The government had sent its notorious constabulary forces to make sure that the dam was built. The left - leaning revolutionaries exploited this issue to the hilt and promised that they would side with us in this fight. And just like Father Balweg, our culture and traditions were so different from that of the rebels, but we had little choice.

I was a teenager when I first started serving the revolution. That is me on the left.

As a teenager, I first served as a courier of top secret messages from Father Balweg — who was later known as Ka Ambo — to his field commanders and tribal allies. We were natural undercover messengers. Though our mountainous region had by then been riddled with Army and constabulary camps and checkpoints, the troops never suspected us, young girls, to be bearing encrypted messages every time we passed by their camps when we went back to our schools on Mondays. I could not imagine the happiness of every message recipient every time I delivered an inspiring letter from Ka Ambo, who was fast becoming a local idol, a Robin Hood of the Cordillera.

I soon dedicated myself fully to the revolution that Father Balweg was leading. I attended lectures that he held at our mountain church. I was very young but I understood and accepted his talk about our tribal right to self – determination. By then, I knew that his main idea was not opposing the construction of the dam that would flood us. Only a few understood it, and I was one of them. We knew that what he wanted all along was autonomy.

By the time I got to take up an education course in Baguio City, I was already a seasoned revolutionary. Though I had not carried any firearms and fired any shot at the enemies, I had seen enough violence and guns in my lifetime. More importantly, because of my quietly professional demeanor, I had already gained the complete trust of the foremost rebel in our tribe's history – Father Conrado Balweg.

There was a period when a massive manhunt was launched to capture – dead or alive – the rebel priest. By then, he and his followers had already executed daring raids on military camps and isolated municipal halls that netted them hundreds of captured government firearms. Attributed to his combat leadership were at least twenty fierce engagements that had claimed the lives of at least fifty government soldiers and members of the militia. In an attempt to put an end to his notoriety, a reward of several hundred thousands of pesos was put out, but the government forces never captured him. All along, I knew where he was hiding – in our little village of Sumadel.

Having been ex-communicated by the church, Ka Ambo soon married a fellow revolutionary, Corazon Cortel. She was young, beautiful and fiery. I had gained her full confidence immediately. I knew that catering to the demands of the quest for Cordillera autonomy would be a lifelong struggle. Being one of the most trusted confidants of the Balweg couple also took heavy demands on my time and lifestyle. I decided that I would never marry and instead fully commit myself to the difficult quest for self-determination: at best, the grant for federal-like autonomy.

Father Balweg, more popularly known as Ka Ambo, was a charismatic leader.

The defining moment of my life came in 1986 when the former president Cory Aquino forged a peace pact with our group. By then, our collective decision was to break away from the communist rebellion that we had joined for seven years. The rebels who hailed mostly from the lowlands, wanted to overthrow the national government before they could start resolving our Cordillera tribal problem. But the hardcore tribal rebels felt otherwise. If the national government was willing to offer them autonomy right away, why engage in this rebellion?

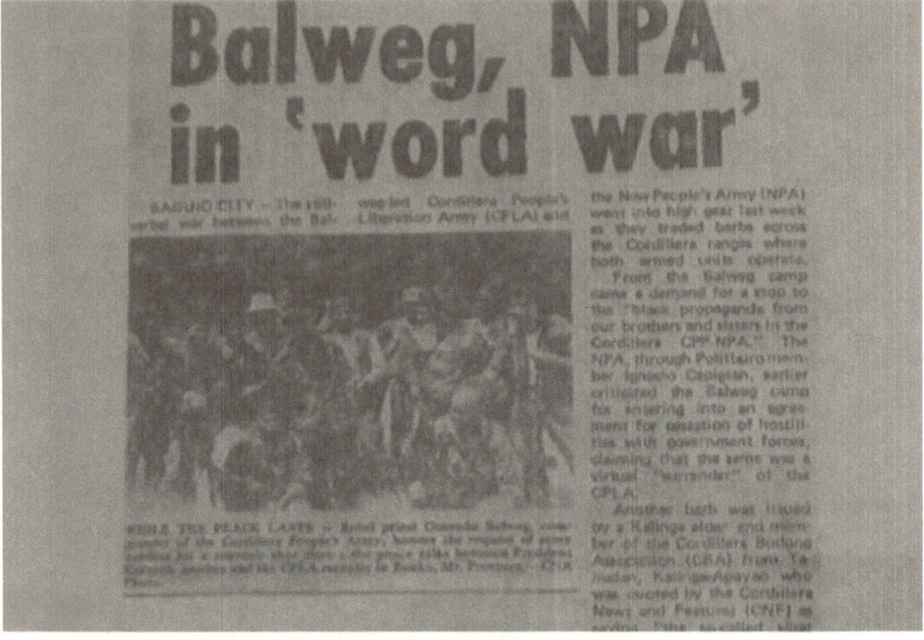

We broke away from the mainstream rebels to form our own Cordillera Peoples' Liberation Army.

We were branded as traitors by the New People's Army when we broke away from them, bringing with us hundreds of firearms to form our Cordillera People's Liberation Army (CPLA). I was part of that core body that organized this fledgling army. What made matters better this time was that we were recognized by the government. While our former comrades put out a death sentence for Father Balweg, we still enjoyed the liberty of pursuing our new found victory — the creation of the Cordillera Administrative Region. I accompanied Father Balweg and his wife whenever there were sessions held to explain the concept of autonomy to our fellow tribesmen. We literally made the road our home as we hopped from one village to another. He was tireless but very happy as he rallied his beloved people to support autonomy. Because of his usual charismatic way, he would get into a village and approach the village elder. His wife, a few bodyguards and I would then weave our way into the village women as Father Balweg charmed his way into getting the support of the elders. He clearly was in his element.

We spent countless days on the road to explain the autonomy we wanted.

But he was assassinated on New Year's Eve four years later. His brother, who was rebel commander of the rival New People's Army, sought a meeting with Father Balweg. An altercation ensued and out of the bushes rang a shot in the dead of night. The father of the Cordillera Revolution was hit on the head. His brother will forever be blamed for the crime. Having been the Balweg couple's most trusted friend and the chief of staff of his office at that time, I was devastated by such news. But it was his wife who was most affected and did not know how to pick up the pieces after his untimely death. Mrs. Balweg and I found solace in embracing and re-affirming the legacy of Ka Ambo's dreams a few weeks later. We dedicated ourselves to pursuing the principles of the peace pact with the government. For us, it was our way of showing our sincere solidarity with the Armed Forces. As a further proof of earnestness, we managed to convince one of the slain rebel priest's sons to become an officer of the Philippine Army. With Mrs. Balweg and a few other loyal supporters, we asked that the former top leaders of our underground group be commissioned as Army officers.

We built a school to further educate our comrades and their children.

With the help of the government, we made education accessible to our former combatants, most of whom did not finish high school. It was a tiring job, but it was our only way of keeping the flame of ka Ambos' dreams alive.

Then, Mrs. Balweg suddenly passed away. She succumbed to medical complications before she could see the fruit of her effort and love for her people. I was again devastated.

There has been an exodus of members with leaders claiming their own factions since. I can never claim to have the same charismatic power as the Balweg couple but in my own little way, just like when I was a teenager forty years ago, I continue to help the struggle. I teach at the school that we built with the military. I teach our combatants' children. After all, they are our future.

Ms. Juanita Chulsi
Longtime assistant to rebel priest

A Good Daughter

My entire family had high hopes for me. My mother expected me to bail our family out of poverty. We were a very poor family from Bulacan, and I considered it as a blessing when the vice mayor took me in as a part time staff while I was studying.

My grandparents were particularly proud of me because I showed promise as a student leader. Owing a debt of gratitude to the town official who partially sponsored my education, I was gradually drawn into his inner circle of friends who all belonged to an underground organization. At first, I did not mind tagging along whenever they organized rallies and went to schools. They protested tuition fee increases. It was a legitimate concern indeed because for the poor students like me, another tuition fee increase meant more sacrifice for our parents.

Because I was a good speaker, I was soon asked to be a regular member of their core group. At first, I resisted because I wanted to focus on my work and studies. Though the pay was not as good, at seventeen, I was already able to bring home some money for food and medicine of my grandparents. It was fulfilling to share, no matter how small the amount I was able to give my family. What made me hopeful was the prospect of finishing college and getting a decent job. My family was really counting on me.

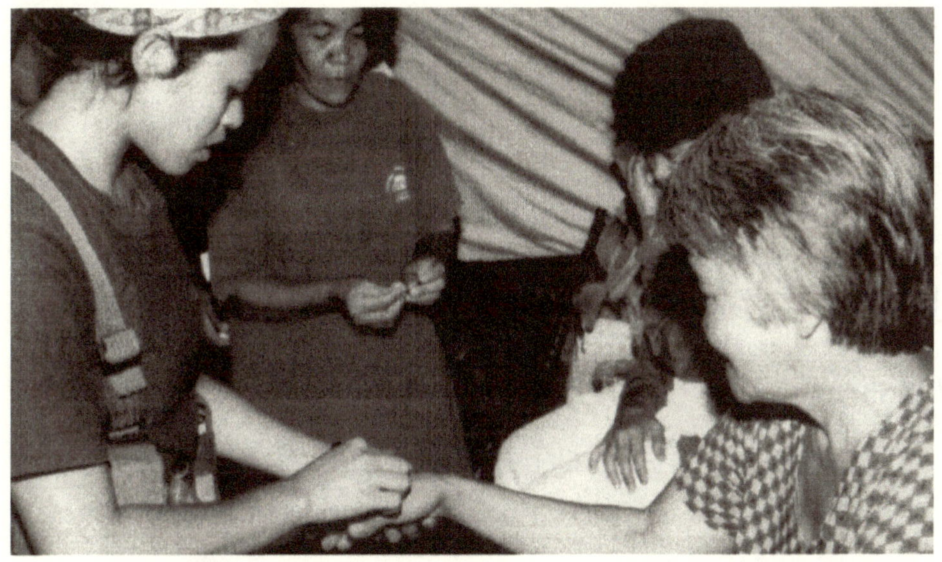

I was initially inspired by the prospect of truly helping people.

But my subsequent decisions failed my family's dreams. I do not know what got into me, but I agreed to attend a primary course for activists.

"You will learn a lot from the course," encouraged one of the vice mayor's friends.

"You will appreciate the true history of the country in this short course, not the ones they teach you in school," she added. Before I knew it, I was already an eager student of the course that presented an alternative view of the Philippine situation. It emphasized how unreliable our government was, especially because it allowed foreigners to exploit our natural resources. Then, I made my decision.

"I am resigning from my job," I declared. My mother was stunned. The money I gave her regularly meant so much to her and the family.

"I want to fight for the oppressed," I added. My mother was completely speechless.

My life changed after that. I soon missed classes because I attended secret organizing sessions. I missed my exams and eventually dropped out of college a year before graduation.

That broke my mother's and grandparents' hearts.

"I am no longer your daughter. I am now a daughter of the oppressed," I declared. My mother must have thought I was possessed. I began to embrace the teachings of the movement. That included learning to detach myself from the family. I guess, it was youthful idealism that made it easy for me.

"Your life now belongs to the motherland," they told me. I felt some sense of self-importance with that remark from my comrades.

I poured my heart and soul into the revolution.

Jobless, I influenced others to join me. Our part in Bulacan has a large number of factories manufacturing everything from electronic parts, machines, umbrellas almost everything you can imagine. Our area drew strength from the money that flowed through the local economy when workers were paid wages. Though their salaries were not always high, they got by. But no revolution succeeds when the people have jobs and are happy, so they must be agitated. Our mission, mine specially, was to open their minds and sabotage the factories. When these close, the economy is crippled, the people become unhappy, so they will rise up in arms. That was the general plan I was to execute.

I was really good at it because I had five factories shut down. I did not mind the thousands of workers that lost their jobs. I did not think about the children who would have to stop school because their parents suddenly lost their jobs. All I thought about was the need to open their eyes.

Our *modus operandi* was simple. All we had to do was organize unions in factories where there was none yet. In establishments that already had a union, we made sure that we had secret cells within the unions themselves. Then we pressured them to demand higher and higher wages. No employee ever rejected the option to demand higher wages.

We took a cut of 10% to 15% of the total amount in the collective bargaining agreement between the management and the unions. But in many instances, a factory owner would rather close down and relocate to another country when confronted with such a situation. And each departure made the country less and less attractive to investors, which was exactly what we wanted.

In my subsequent activities as an instructor of other armed rebels, I soon met and fell in love with the man of my dreams. Though he was not handsome, I liked the fire in his eyes whenever he talked about encircling the cities from the countryside. Like me, he was completely sold on the ideology we espoused. Our union soon bore a child.

Then, he gave in to the temptations of another female fighter. Our kids were still so young when I left him. It was painful but I could not tolerate his infidelity. My circumstances forced me to lie low and ask for a leave of absence from the movement.

Life became a very serious challenge when my marriage to a comrade broke up.

Life was definitely hard as a single mother. My kids never knew who their real father was. I had no pictures of him and did not want to keep any in our house. Life was really hard. It was only when I was in dire need of money for my children's milk that I realized how much sadness and misery I caused parents who lost their jobs when we successfully had a factory close down. When we rejoiced at yet another factory shut down, thousands grieved.

I survived scraping off the revolutionary tax collections that I was eventually assigned to gather. I became good at it too because I knew how the money flow went.

But I was captured by the military. At first, I thought I was going to be harmed and maybe, even killed. I was lucky to have been caught by a unit whose commander realized how bad my situation was as a single mother.

"We are willing to help you if you have truly decided to start over again," he assured me. It would have been nineteen years in 2009 since I became an activist and left school. For the sake of my children, I accepted the Army commander's offer to be enlisted in the Army. I encourage the youth to avoid the mistakes I made by sharing my experience and the lessons I learned. And just like before, I find joy in my new vocation.

Corporal Angel Reyes
Former rebel organizer

Confronting God in My Prison

As a consequence of what we did in "Oakwood," in 2003 more than three hundred officers and men were incarcerated and numerous others held in restriction for being involved. If one counts the number of families and dependents these soldiers have, the number of those affected could easily shoot up to thousands. Considering that we have not achieved our goal of reforming the AFP, the suffering of the concerned officers and men including their families are not worth it. It will only be worthy if indeed the objectives of reform were attained. In this particular case, the answer is obvious. From my perspective as a detainee, I kept asking this question: Is imprisonment a result of the incident or is it something predestined so that I could have the opportunity to reflect and reform myself?

Becoming a bitter person and focusing on the elements of hate is a matter of choice. Becoming a better individual is also a matter of choice.

To use one's predicament of being a detainee or a prisoner as a reason for embarking into a tumultuous road of vengeance and bitterness is certainly an option, particularly for someone who believes he was a victim of injustice. The situation is aggravated if that prisoner refuses to see the situation from a perspective other than his. In this case, he tends to see himself as always right and others as always wrong. This can only be overcome if one ceases to see himself as the bastion of "righteousness" and start seeing other views.

I was a combat-seasoned officer before I took part in the Oakwood siege. That is me on the right.

We detainees could be categorized into three groups: those who are guilty, those who are innocent and those who are likewise guilty but refuse to acknowledge it. The third group sees the "wrong" done to them but never the wrongs they have done.

As military officers detained, acknowledging our mistake is difficult. In fact, it is a painful process particularly if pride and ego are at stake. Often times, we just want to forget about it and just bury that thought. It is too self- demeaning to accept that we have committed a mistake especially if we always think that we are right.

However, this mindset is wrong because it is pride that fuels it. It would be better if our actions are driven by humility and consideration of other perspectives. The hard stance by military officers can only be corrected through intense reflection which could eventually lead to genuine self- transformation.

As military officers, we were used to calling the shots in our respective units which made us feel we are always in control. But that is not the situation inside the detention cell. We may have an idea as to how to do things but the consequences are not always to our liking — nor our expectations.

It was an abrupt change, from a virtual somebody to a nobody. We want to do something but we cannot. We want to spend time with our family visiting us, but there is not enough time because visiting hours is limited to 3 hours. Such visitation rules, of course, vary and are dependent on the detention facility's policy.

Before incarceration, we had the whole world was for us to move around and enjoy. Inside detention, we got to spend twenty four hours inside a four-by-five-meter cell. We needed to ask permission just to see sunlight, yet seeing the sun could only last for an hour. We do it while we are in handcuffs or placed behind a barbed wire under the watchful eyes of our guards. In some detention facilities, babies had to be passed through a tiny gap of concertina wire just for the detained fathers to hug them. Worse, these restrictions are imposed by guards who are fellow soldiers themselves, telling us each time that they were simply doing their job. Before, we were in control, but now we are put under control.

The situation inside detention initially made me angry, bitter and hateful. In fact, there were times when I just gnashed my teeth in frustration because things do not happen my way. I was in despair. I was no longer in control, in stark contrast to the time I was a commanding officer or a platoon leader of an infantry rifle unit. That was the bottom line and this made me feel so helpless.

During the first few months of detention, I was ruled by my anger. A detainee could do things such as throwing bottles at the guards, punching people, shouting at a senior officer, and trying to engage in a fistfight. This attitude predominated perhaps as an unconscious defense mechanism against the painful reality that one is no longer in control. True enough, the hate and rebellious spirit lasted months until helplessness again came in.

Oftentimes, the feeling of helplessness is considered as something negative. One simply has to do something about his being helpless, something which could lead to his demise, particularly if he is not in a righteous path. A military officer bringing his men into a public place with arms is definitely not a righteous act.

I had everything going well for my career before we took part in
military adventurism. That is me on the right.

However, I realized that the feeling of helplessness should not be necessarily considered as something negative. In fact, it could lead to humility. It is just a matter of choice whether one, in his helplessness, allows himself to reflect or decides to become more rebellious. Incarceration can lead to a once in a lifetime opportunity to genuinely reflect on what has happened and hopefully, pave the way to become a better person. It could also lead a man to become a full time rebel. In the end however, it is a matter of choice. Detention can indeed either make a military officer more humble or angrier. It is a choice either to harbor bitterness, respond in anger and be carried away by methodologies of hate or to allow transformational spirit to come-in and go on with life with love and peace in one's heart.

It was hard to pick up life inside a military detention facility. It seemed that life has stalled. Life had ceased to go on. At the back of a detainee's mind, life will only be restored upon freedom from the bondage of incarceration. You pretend that things are normal, but in reality it is not. It is the struggle between abnormality and normalcy of life that often times occupy the minds of prisoners. But sometimes detention does not only last for a few weeks and months. It could last for years especially with the kind of justice system in the country. Coping mechanisms will have to be undertaken, which varies for different individuals. True reflection in life will set-in often times jumpstarted by spiritual beliefs as harmonized with family affairs and manifested through activities inside detention which are often entrepreneurial in nature. The spirit, mind and heart must be cleared.

As we spent time inside the Custodial Management Unit of the Philippine Army, it turned out that picking up life is not that hard after all. It started when church workers from different Christian churches began to minister to us. At first it was a difficult struggle because pride and arrogance were all over the rebellious-minded officers. The church workers would endure snubs and harsh treatments from some of the officers who were detained as they persevered to bring the gospel inside detention.

I rediscovered myself after my long years in detention. That is me
at the center.

But God has His purpose and He will not be denied. During those trying times, Pastor Vic Tigas a former General turned Pastor from the Friends of Jesus Christ Ministries came. It was easy for him to connect to us because he himself was detained and was in fact, a retired military officer. Aside from Pastor Vic, many Christian workers came and eventually became regular visitors conducting bible studies and other spiritual activities. Who ever they were, wherever they came from, was not an issue. The point is in listening to the message through Bible studies. It is the Message and not the Messenger.

Pastor Vic started conducting Bible studies in the Intelligence Service Armed Forces of the Philippines Detention Center in 2004, where I have been an attendee. It continued until the time I was transferred to the Custodial Management Unit of the Philippine Army in Fort Bonifacio. During that time, many officers at CMU were already regular Bible study attendees of Pastor Vic's ministry work.

The period when spiritual devotions were at hand had been the key for many officers to rediscover their relationship with God. It paved the way for us to realize that it is all right to pick up life once again. Life need not stall. No matter where one is and whatever situation he is in, it is the Spiritual Freedom that provides peace and brings back normalcy as it takes away the rebellious spirit.

Since then, spiritual and church activities became regular together with the Christian service conducted by the Friends of Jesus Christ Ministries on Saturday mornings and the Catholic Mass in the afternoons. A spiritual fellowship developed inside the detention facility and members had their regular schedule for praise and worship as well as singing rehearsals. Prayer was done in a 24-hour continuous cycle. The fellowship was called CMUCF or the Custodial Management Unit Christian Fellowship. Transformation for each and every individual officer inside the Army detention had been obvious no matter what religion or sect or spiritual affiliations they initially had.

The former rebellious minded officers slowly transformed into spiritual-minded beings. The tenet of submitting to authority because God allows every authority to exist, otherwise He disallows it, became clear to us. This realization is not easy for those of us who have relied so much on our own understanding of how to perform our duties and responsibilities as Army officers.

But God works in mysterious ways. Sometimes He "punishes" a person or places him in a helpless situation so much so that he does not have any recourse but to remember Him and go back to Him. God has his own ways of giving a person the opportunity to reignite his relationship with Him. He loves each of us so much that when the time comes and He knocks on our hearts, all we need to do is respond in accordance to His Will. It is a matter of allowing Him to take charge. Such situations, where, more often than not become the turning point in a man's life, most often come in the most difficult and trying times. It is in a man's lowest times and most helpless situations that God will be at work.

That is me on the left, with my wartime buddies in the all-out war against the separatists in 2000. The author is on the right.

This was the case for many of the so called Magdalo Officers who were detained. With God's grace, many responded. It only shows that no matter how tough a person is, no matter how many battles he has fought, he is still nothing without the loving grace of his Creator. Many CMU detainees understood this.

Though I have a distinct and quite different perspective of religious beliefs, I believe that finding the way towards a personal relationship with God Almighty is what matters most. Regardless of a person being a "Christian," an "INC," a "Catholic" or whatever religious affiliation he may possess, it is God who will ultimately be the judge of one's spiritual worthiness.

I have learned a very important lesson in life with my experience in 2003 and my detention in particular. Being a Ranger or an Army officer with the self perception of being among those soldiers who suffer in the frontlines does not give me the right to be the bastion of righteousness and feel like the ultimate provider of solutions to the nation's problems. Not even excellent performance of duty can justify soldiers intervening in political affairs. In the process, my companions and I ended up pawns of individuals and groups with covert political agenda.

Today, I run a small NGO that extends helpful reach to poor children.

But I have no ill feeling against these people. Whatever my participation was, I stand to face it and answer for whatever consequences it may bring. I can not blame others for what I went thru because my participation was my personal decision and I am responsible for it. It's a pity I cannot do much for those I influenced and who did join me in my adventure. It haunts me, but God knows I have done everything I could, especially for the troops.

Such a grand objective of correcting society is not a matter to be decided by a few individuals or a group. As human beings, we can only do so much. In reforming the AFP, we have to start from ourselves and it should be done from within the organization. It has to start from little things and if great and bigger things are bestowed upon us by the Will of God, it will come to pass in accordance to His Will.

Reform has to start from within each and every one of us. It has to be deeply rooted from within.

I have found peace and joy in life.

Captain Milo Maestrecampo
Magdalo group key leader

(This story was personally written by Captain Maestrecampo while he was in detention.)

Tribal Fighters

I came from a poor family. Five of my siblings had stopped going to school as my parents could no longer afford it. I was fifteen when I asked the Catholic Church in our parish to take me in.

In 1975, nobody in North Cotabato knew about the communist-inspired rebels yet. But the five priests who eventually sought shelter in our church where I was the errand boy had something to do with the growth and expansion of the insurgency in Mindanao.

"Collect three cups of rice and two pesos from each house daily," ordered one of the five priests.

I dutifully obliged, and for two years, I did not even question where the money went. I had become a collector for the priests.

"They will be for the people in the mountains," one priest said. I did not question them until I was told that the local police chief had been closely monitoring a young kid collecting revolutionary taxes. That was me! I was a teenage revolutionary tax collector without my knowing it. I was depressed.

I was only seventeen when I became a full-time rebel.

I officially started my 24-year rebel adventure when I was seventeen. For fear of my life, I ran to the rebels, who were then a very small group. I eventually came to work closely with Commander Benzar and Commander Parago. These two are still active rebels. They joined the movement only 2 years before I did but they were so good at intimidating people — even their own comrades!

They knew where I was good at — collecting revolutionary tax — and they loved me for it.

We would approach store owners to ask for small donations like one kilo of rice or sugar, a pack of cigarettes or coffee. Then, they become part of the regular collection route until we are able to assess how much revolutionary tax to impose on them the way government tax collectors do. Unlike them however, we carried guns to the store owners paid. At some point, we began ransacking small stores for the goods we needed.

We preyed even on the farmers. We were told that we should not steal anything from the masses, not even the smallest needle. Yet, we destroyed their crops if the farmers did not give their small but regular contributions.

But we loved the bigger businesses because they knew they could lose more than the amount we were demanding. So they all paid up.

As regards the huge banana plantations in our area, the trick was simple. We chopped down hectares of land planted to bananas or threatened to insert needles in their bananas. To avoid the risk of losing their lucrative export businesses if their buyers complained about needles in the bananas, they paid us revolutionary tax.

Bus companies that plied the highways were much easier to convince. We always demanded large sums from these companies. If they did not pay up, which was often rare, we simply burned one of their buses. That always brought home the point.

I benefited from these collections but not as nicely as our commanders. From these collections, the movement sponsored the education of my two kids who were sent to Cebu as true scholars of the revolution. Our fighters also got a regular allowance, small but better than nothing. The common system was to match a store with a rebel. We demand, not ask them, to send the rebels' family, 1,200 pesos monthly instead of paying us the revolutionary taxes. Our contacts in the cities and towns would link up the poor small store owners who sustained the family of a rebel. I wondered what service we rendered the village entrepreneurs who were also barely able to make a living.

Tribal people made up 80% of our ranks. We told them that we were their real army. Most of these indigenous people were illiterate, nomadic mountain farmers. We would help them with their farm chores, fix their poultry cages, help with their fish ponds, or any chore that would endear us to them. When they have conflicts and issues, we gave swift justice. We got their sympathy and support.

We controlled the tribal people and had them run errands for us.

The tribal peoples ran errands for us. They hardly questioned our motives. Of course, it also helped that we shared a few pesos of the revolutionary taxes we collected.

But we also struck fear in them when they did not cooperate. As early as the recruitment stage, while winning them over to become regular armed rebels, we would convince them that the time to act and bear arms could not wait. We would tell them that they must not wait for the day when the military will just gun them down. Many believed us, and readily joined. Those who did not were often identified or tagged as our sympathizers so they would seek our help whenever they sensed that the military was hot on their tails.

But beyond all these, what slowly opened my eyes was the utter ruthlessness of two major figures in the Davao area insurgency:

Commander Benzar and Commander Parago.

I worked closely with two of the most ruthless rebel commanders.

Parago does not choose whom to kill and whom to spare. He actually made a name in the bloody Digos massacre where he ordered the execution of an entire village — men, women, children, all of whom he suspected as cooperating with the military than them. The sheer number of innocent victims and the manner by which they were systematically executed as their families pleaded made national headlines.

Benzar is equally fearsome. When one recruit refuses to join him, he simply shoots him in front of his family. Anybody who resists joining his band, he kills mercilessly. That is the reason why he has so many followers.

Both seem paranoid. In Paquibato district in Davao City, which Parago calls his kingdom, a fish vendor passed him by. In his native language, he called out loudly "Buy some fish!" Parago suspected him of being a look out for the military. He had the poor vendor killed in plain sight of civilians. He killed a lot of people that way. For me, the worst thing that he did was killing wounded comrades. He did not want the inconvenience of caring for the wounded nor the risk of capture if we had them hospitalized. That did not sit well with me.

Our leader took on wearing military uniforms as he terrorized the people.

I got tired, and casually approached my commander to allow me to leave.

"I have served the people for twenty four years," I told him.

"I am tired," I said. I could not tell him that we all claimed to save the people from their problems yet I could not save my own family and solve my personal problems.

"How can I help others when I cannot help myself," I thought.

"I am already old," I told him. But, I somehow wanted a new life. I wanted to leave the dangerous path those five priests led me to when I was fifteen.

I went down and surrendered to the authorities. That was the boldest decision I have ever made because our leaders always said that we will be killed if we gave up.

"Come join us in the fight," invited the military commander.

"The tribal leaders are asking us for their protection if they launched a counter attack against the rebels." Somehow, that struck me as strange because I was used to seeing them so obedient - no complaints, no gripes, just determined fighters.

"Would you be able to help them?" the commander asked.

Our rebel leaders abused the tribal people.

And the memories of the abuse against them came back to me.

"Yes, I will lead," I declared, all my pent up anger at the way we treated them.

I led a pack of fully armed former rebels and legions of

indigenous people. They liked the confidence that I put in them. After all, they have also seen me fight throughout the years that I was a revolutionary cadre. With expert native skill, we hunted our former comrades. And with every victory against them, I went on radio to announce that our group was going to do more against their abuses. I felt like a general rallying his army to counter-attack.

I was soon hunted by my former comrades for leading the fight against them. But I did not mind. Here was the former teenage revolutionary tax collector who had seen it all and who has now come to regret what he did. And just like the Crusades, I saw myself

Loreto Palma
Davao insurgent since the 1970's

For Our Children

Teach-ins and a progression of trainings and indoctrinations instill in our minds beliefs and mindsets — even ways of speaking — a peculiar vocabulary with matching pessimism.

Constant reminders of three evils - feudalism, capitalism and imperialism and how issues must be understood and interpreted in light of these evils.

The political and organizational initiatives of the cadre had always relied on these. The military on the other hand, responded at first with force using cannons, highly trained troops and helicopter bombings. Later they also trained to go for the hearts and minds of the people. Their effort and sacrifices delivered mere dents to our strength and motivations. The military force that was applied against us actually increased our numbers. Whenever one of us was hurt, two or three among the people — friends and family — would replace the casualty.

When the military first used their new pro-people approach, they began to gain ground. Most popular was the Army Literacy Patrol System or ALPS, an alternative learning system. Two soldiers taught the alphabet to the villagers. We had difficulty finding a match for it in our campaigns. These teacher-soldiers not only had a positive attitude, they brought good news and they struck at the core of our propaganda. We were so glad when we found out that the program was discontinued.

The military came against us with highly-trained troops like
the Scout Rangers.

But what really destroyed the revolution was not simply the military right-hand and left-hand approach programs that struck us as a group. The other initiatives that targeted our individual psyches were the most effective.

The first one that I truly admired was a regular radio program run by the Cagayan Governor in 1980s, former Constabulary Colonel Rodolfo Aguinaldo. He would identify our family members through his vast networks of former rebels that volunteer to serve him. He would then have these family members ask their relatives to surrender voluntarily.

"Son, we know you are not safe in the mountains. Please come home now," a mother would tearfully call her son. So many among the rebels would relate to this station even if it were not their own mother speaking on the radio.

"I love you very much, I do not want you to die in the jungle," the mother would say.

"The soldiers will treat you well, if you come down," a mother would assure him. Among the rebels in our group, it was actually the fear of being abused by the constabulary and Army that prevented them from leaving the movement. Our leaders warn us that we will be tortured if we surrendered to the police.

But it was different when it was my child I heard over the radio. I was surprised when one day, while we were cleaning our rifles inside our secret camp, I heard the voice of my child over the radio.

"Papa and mama, please come down now," my daughter was starting to cry.

My heart was melting when I heard her voice.

"I am sick, please come down," she pleaded, in her frail and sickly voice.

Her mother, my wife, was also listening beside me. We found true love in the mountains, among rebels. I was just a new recruit then, not even two years in the movement. She joined the movement even later. Yet, it seemed to have been love at first sight. Smitten, I started courting her immediately and that was when I got my first disciplinary action punishment from the party.

Our rules forbid courting a fellow revolutionary unless he has spent at least two years with the group. More importantly, one who has a romantic interest in a fellow fighter must get the permission of the party first before he could start courting. I violated both because of love.

I suffered through that period but because I was such a reliable warrior, my punishment was soon lifted even before my time was up.

My wife was soon pregnant and just like revolutionary wives, she spent her months expecting inside the comfort of our desolate camp — that mountain fortress that we thought was so secure that even pregnant women and recovering casualties felt safe there.

"Where do we bring the baby?" she asked me after she gave birth

It was forbidden to have children in camp to maintain mobility.

"Let us leave her with a relative," I told her. Back then, as it is now, we left our children with our parents, relatives or supporters. We, dedicated fighters, then resumed our work in the mountains.

My wife was as committed to the revolution as I was.

"They will take care of her well. They have to," I reassured my wife. She was as committed to the rebellion as I was. During those times, she would not even consider going home for a few days or weeks just to take care of our child. To her, our daughters' life was important but service to the people was even more important.

We delivered our newborn daughter to a relative, just like delivering a sack of rice to a buyer. She was crying when we left her.

"I will take care of her," our relative declared. My wife did not know how sincere she was. It was possible that she was just afraid to reject our request for fear of her life. Whatever her reason was, we left our baby with her without leaving a single peso for her to buy milk or medicines.

At the expense of our daughter's future, my wife and I became committed revolutionaries.

Then off we went. We both believed that we were depriving our daughter of something so important, yet, we were selflessly serving the revolution-without pay. We dreamt about how our kid would have looked after several years of our absence. That is why it came as a surprise when we first heard her angelic voice over the radio asking us to surrender.

We had been irresponsible parents for so long. My wife and I agreed to surrender, even if our leaders did not allow us. We had no offense against the revolution; in fact, we had been both loyal fighters for almost a decade.

When we saw our daughter for the first time, both of us were joyously excited. We had seen the real fruit of our sacrifice -in the innocent eyes of our daughter. She eventually recovered from her illness, and my wife has not gone back to the mountain since.

I was pleasantly surprised when a few more of our comrades also surrendered after we did. They too had loved ones -wives, mothers, children -who had been waiting for their return.

Eduardo Jose
Rebel in Cagayan Valley
in the 1980s

Starting Over

I occasionally bump into my former comrades. Some of them are still active insurgents, while others like me, have gone on with their lives. With hopes for a new life, those of us who have given up our arms have taken different paths. Some have gone back to farming, some opted for jobs in the city while others have become entrepreneurs. As for me, I became a public servant.

For ten years, I tried doing different things, but almost always failed. Then, I tried running for office as village chief. Apparently, the people still wanted me to serve because I won!

Even when I was young, I always regarded public service as something to aspire for. I was a student activist in college and held positions in several clubs and organizations, most of which were left-leaning and definitely radical. I was forced to become a full-time partisan after the city – based subversive organization I was part of was exposed and labeled a threat to the civic order. When a manhunt for us was launched, I was welcomed by the communist-inspired movement. It was the most convenient choice for me but one that took over my life for the next 6 years.

I loved organizing people and helping them become self-reliant.

I enjoyed agitating them for collective action. I burned into their minds an image of a beautiful country where everyone was educated. A good part of my audience were illiterates who have opted to remain so because the nearest schools were too far away.

I loved teaching the rural youth the basic lessons in rebellion.

But they eagerly listened to our propaganda and believed that education was not the national government's priority. When we told them that more money was spent on bullets than books, they became angry. Recruiting them was easy!

Our recruits had simple dreams. Many wanted to go to school, something we promised would be made available to everybody when we win. They wanted land and we said we'd give them that. They wanted livelihood, and we said we will provide job opportunities. We did not know exactly how, but we promised to give them all that.

Our recruits were mostly male but there were several women who also volunteered and were willing to die for the revolution as well!

We built a network of camps much like the ones Vietnam had.

Tunnels and underground bunkers were built in the mountains of Mabiga in Apayao. The enthusiasm of the younger rebels was written in their faces as they dug the tunnels and made fortifications. I must have inspired them with my idealism. They worked hard and long hours to fortify what became the most impregnable rebel camp in the country.

The military came at us in waves. They pounded us with heavy howitzer fires for days on end. Our ears were bleeding from all the explosions but there was no moving us out of our territory. The armed forces launched helicopter rocket attacks, for weeks on end. We simply shrugged these off, convinced that we will prevail.

It was hard fighting the combat-seasoned Scout Rangers.

At one point, we knew we had the tactical advantage over the Philippine Army. We repelled several attacks by infantry forces. Our vast network of booby traps and improvised explosive devices where simply too much for them.

"What can you do for us now, Ka Brix?" asked a new surrenderee. I was dumbfounded because I honestly did not have a ready answer anymore. It was easy to rouse people to see the problem but it was much, much harder to come up with a solution.

After much thought, I decided to turn to those I once considered my archenemies: the government forces.

We bolted out of the revolution because it was no longer responsive
to our needs.

I proposed that the government focus less on military combat operations and let the Army do more livelihood-oriented service. I was convinced them that any government counter insurgency must target the root causes first. Poverty and ignorance were clearly on top. But I had reservations as to how exactly the former rebels would be welcomed back as productive members of society.

The hindrances to their successful re integration to normal society were huge. The government had allocated a measly sum for each rebel returnee to subsist on for at most a week. While there were plans to teach them how to earn, these plans never really took off.

It was difficult to teach entrepreneurial skills to the warriors who have known only the ways of the mountains.

I wished that the military could help the rebel returnees craft a financial blue print for themselves. I became frustrated because at that time, the soldiers was as battle weary as we were. While they were sworn to protect the citizenry, they were also expected to help in nation-building. But the long drawn-out insurgency has sharply focused the soldier on the key skills that assured his survival: fine marksmanship and the art of killing. The skill set needed by the soldier to inspire a rebel towards a vibrant and productive entrepreneur life remained undeveloped.

Deep inside, I knew that the rebels could head back to the mountains once more, if they were not sufficiently assisted and mentored.

I did not want to fail their expectations, but most indicators showed that my efforts were going southward. It had been another year since I began hoping for a comprehensive program that would build productive skill sets in former rebels. I had stayed in my position as village chief but my achievements had been less than significant.

I was very happy in 2010 when the military embraced a more holistic approach to their counter insurgency operations. While their metrics for success relied on enemy body count and captured enemy firearms, the military has learned its lesson. It can only win the war if it involved the stakeholders. Having seen the futility of relying purely on combat prowess to conquer the enemy, they have correctly identified the root causes of rebellion as the main enemy. I was also happy when a band of Army engineers, in partnership with a local media-based foundation, started building a school in the area that I serve. I saw the enthusiasm of the soldiers and I shared the deepest appreciation of the community for that new school. We waited long for this and I hope more will come.

Jose Piñera
Rebel commander in Kalinga
in the 1980's

Losing My Sons

My father was not afraid to lose me. I grew up in a family where daughters were not as prized as the sons.

"They would all go away to marry anyway," my father would always say.

"They are of no use to our family. They will only serve their husbands."

My father never encouraged us to finish school. Only two of my sisters finished high school while the rest of us did not even complete elementary level. I felt as though my father wished we would all just go away.

So, it was no big deal when I married at sixteen. And because my father was not a role model, I did not know how to raise a family.

To make matters worse, I married an irresponsible man. Just like my father, he was a farmer. But unlike my father, he was an alcoholic.

"We do not have money anymore to buy you gin," I would chide him. But while he did not always have the energy to find food for me and our first-born son, he somehow managed to produce a few pesos to buy his drinks.

I escaped my horrible married life into the waiting arms of the revolution.

"Just join the revolution full time and your problems will be solved," the rebel recruiter told me.

"You have such a difficult family life with a husband like that," she said. I was confused because I wanted to escape my husband's irresponsible behavior, yet I did not want to lose my son.

"We are the only solution to your problem. The rebel movement will take care of your son's education," she continued.

I decided to become a full time rebel. Soon after I made my decision, I knew I was going to lose my family. I was first given the task of organizing farmers. It was a fulfilling job indeed to rally farmers and try to help solve their problems. Land reform was most urgent. Sometimes even siblings killed each other because of rival claims on a piece of ancestral land. A few times, there were unscrupulous land grabbers who would take the law into their own hands. We summarily killed these characters. But while I found fulfillment in the revolutionary cause, my problems at home were worsening.

I left my son in the care of my in-laws. They soon hated me for that. But the only reason I wanted to join the rebellion was to provide a better future for my son.

My husband tried to renew ties with me. Somehow, I welcomed it because I still loved him despite his shortcomings. Despite me being a full time rebel in hiding, our reconciliation bore another son. I had to leave my new born son again with my in-laws, who resented it. I just wanted to stay away from my husband, but I deeply loved my sons. My own father would have anything to do with me or my children.

I was sent in first to make sure the venues of secret meetings were safe.

I never really joined any armed confrontations against the military. However, I was a trusted organizer of clandestine activities. When our group needed to move to another base, I would be sent in first to reconnoiter the proposed relocation site. When there was a major rebel gathering, and there were two significant ones every year, I was there first at the secret location, making sure that all the administrative arrangements were taken care of. In the course of doing my mostly administrative underground work, I transferred from one place to another. Despite my sacrifice, I did not receive the promised help for my two sons.

Just as we were losing the revolution, I was also losing my sons. When I visited them one time, my eldest, then seven years old, said something that I will never forget: "We do not have a mother."

It pained me to hear that. And I knew I had lost my sons.

But I had duties to perform as a revolutionary.

"Let us recover the areas that we have lost," ordered my commander.

And because I wanted to escape the pain of having heard my son say that they had no mother, I went all out on my rebel work again.

We have lost the affection of the people because nothing among our promises materialized. They would no longer cooperate with us because by then, the military had already gotten to them. They would no longer feed us the way they used to.

We took to raising our own rice supply. Since we did not want to die of hunger, we cultivated our own rebel rice fields. I then realized that what we had been doing whenever we asked for food from those very poor people, we burdened them even more. But now that the military secured them, the people already had refused to give us food.

And, like the people we vowed to serve, my eldest also rejected me. Time had flown so fast. For fifteen years, I was a faithful cadre but I was also an irresponsible mother for the same length of time. I tried so hard to convince my son to come back, but just like me, my teenage son would rather be a "stowaway."

I feared losing my second son, too. That was when I brought up the idea of giving up for good.

"I am leaving the movement," I told my commander. He just kept silent. I knew how much they would miss a reliable ally like me.

I just left. And with me came my husband. He had also joined me as a rebel, leaving our two sons entirely in the care of his parents.

I do not know what drove him to join me, but his decision tore our family completely apart.

Our second son also ran away from us. I tried to convince him to stay but just like me then, he also felt abandoned. Just when I wanted to regain their love, they rejected me.

I had no money but my husband and I tilled the rice field of his parents until we were able to buy ourselves a water buffalo. My husband, after all the years as rebel, was finally able to buy himself a water buffalo.

I also saved enough to buy myself a sewing machine. I hoped to sew dresses that I would sell in the market. I took pride in my only possession when I finally found my sons.

"We can now live together," I declared.

"I now have a sewing machine and your father now has a water buffalo," I tearfully told my sons.

I had looked forward to their positive reaction.

But they no longer wanted to have anything to do with me. They said they had moved on and can now stand on their own.

I felt so rejected.

"What is there to live for?" I told myself.

I never knew if my father felt the same way when I bolted out of our household, married and hied off to the mountains. Now, only the pain of having lost my sons because of one big mistake remains. Nothing is more painful than losing the very lives I brought in the world.

Erlinda Rosales
Rebel in Samar since 1979

On The Right Side of The Law

I never imagined that moment would come. But there I was, receiving my 2nd lieutenant's bars as the military band played. I would soon be in charge of regular troops. How ironic, I thought. Then again, my life was a patchwork of adventures and misadventures.

I was once a rebel leader. In my ten years with the underground movement from 1976 to 1986, I had proven my battle prowess and my tactical acumen several times. The special unit that I led was noted for specializing in bloody raids against isolated police detachments and municipal town halls. I must have contributed the most number of government firearms to our arsenal than any other rebel commander in the Cordillera region.

We always started by sending an attractive woman to befriend the soldiers or policemen in the camps. Guards were often suspicious of hawkers plying their trade at the gates. Besides, pretending to be a vendor would not take anyone inside the camp. But with females, the police guards let their defenses down. Maybe lonely from the isolation, they would talk to our female intelligence agents, even entertain them and offer snacks inside the camps. They hardly noticed that they were under close scrutiny for an attack.

We carefully planned every raid we did on police detachments.

We began to draft plans as soon as our agents returned. The most important information we needed were the strengths of the detachment, the firearms they have, schedules of activities and the defense layout. Using a clay or soil terrain model of the camp, we would plan what to do. Planning usually took three months but more complicated situations required up to a year of planning. As a standard operating procedure in my rebel unit, I would case the target myself before we launched the attack. I would pretend to be a farmer looking for my lost water buffalo, and the police guards would entertain me inside their camps, not knowing that I was an enemy!

One of my first successful raids against a police outpost was in the town of Balbalan in Kalinga. That was executed so well because we went in so fast and caught all the policemen totally off guard. I was grinning from ear to ear as we carted away with all the firearms in that police station. The guards would rather surrender to us and give away their issued firearms than be killed. We then retreated to our own camp and planned our next raid.

We mercilessly attacked lightly defended militia outposts.

We launched another raid on yet another isolated police station in Mountain Province on a very cold day in January 1985. Again, my plan was bold and audacious. We first prepared the police station that was manned by constabulary men and militias. The defenders put on a token fight. But they knew that they simply were no match to us, the highly motivated attackers.

"Surrender or you will all die!" I shouted on my megaphone after we sufficiently showered the remote police station with bullets.

"We just want your firearms," I clarified our purpose. The constabulary men, all cowering in fear, all came down, with their hands behind the back of their heads. Their warriors' pride disappeared in the face of certain death. We searched the outpost and seized whatever documents contained information we needed. Of course, our greatest accomplishment was carrying away fifty of their firearms. For us, a fledgling group of rebels, that arms cache was valuable. With those firearms, we could launch more daring raids.

Our troops operated in large numbers during our heyday.

I must say we have gained sufficient strength in the mid 1980's to post a direct and potent threat to government forces. At that time, much of the might of the Philippine Army was focused on our highland area of operations. Government troops were ambushed often. Death was a daily occurrence. We also suffered casualties, but we always retaliated with more ferocity every time we lost a comrade. As an aspiring rebel commander, I personally led all the violent attacks on government posts. And in each firefight, blood was spilled. Yet somehow, throughout those rebel years, I did not feel any guilt. All the violence I inflicted on the constabulary men were just my way of showing them the pain that I once suffered in their hands.

In the early 1970's when then President Marcos declared Martial Law, the troops abused their power. I was a teenager at that time and I suffered several beatings in the cruel hands of one particularly harsh constabulary man. He kicked me. Boxed me, got my pair of shoes, my trousers and sent me home in my underwear. That was a completely humiliating experience that drove me to volunteer with the New People's Army as one of their youngest recruits. Having witnessed my proficiency in combat tactics and combat leadership, I was then singled out to be further trained in the finer art of guerilla warfare. But I really did not need so much training in fighting because I belonged to one of the fiercest mountain tribes that had a long head-hunting tradition. My career as a rebel field commander flourished as I started registering victory one after another. I was eventually promoted to command the entire special rebel forces in the Cordillera in 1986. I became the master tactician of the rebel forces. The national leadership of the revolutionary army was all praises at my string of flawlessly executed raids. They entrusted to me all the powerful firearms, the logistics and all other activities in my area. Little did the top rebel leadership know that I had other plans.

In an instant, my fellow highlander rebels in the New People's Army defected from the group we had faithfully served for years. We formed the breakaway Cordillera People's Liberation Army, which sought to fight for autonomy for our mountain region. With our action, our former comrades in the underground declared us their mortal enemies.

Having joined forces with the Philippine Army, I showed the location of the major rebel camps. In one sortie, I showed a clandestine training base where a thousand recruits were being trained. The military commander sent a barrage of howitzer and helicopter rockets into the location I identified. I also encouraged my former subordinates to guide government troops in attacks against our remote camps. I did not know why, but I was consumed by my desire to help government troops who had been fighting the rebels for so long.

And perhaps, as gesture of faith in the peace process that our breakaway group offered, the national government brokered an agreement that offered a most attractive opportunity: the integration of former rebel combatants into the regular forces of the Philippine Army. And perhaps because I was recognized as one of the best tactical commanders of the Cordillera People's Liberation Army, I was offered one of the first few officer commissionship slots.

I enjoyed the training we took as integrees into the Philippine Army.

I had very deep reservations when I was first considered a

potential Philippine Army Officer. I was old at 45 - compared to the young guns from the Philippine Military Academy or the Officer Candidate School. While I had a long list of battle accomplishment under my belt, I was not even a high school graduate, when all my officer contemporaries were certified college graduates. I lacked the refinement and sophistication of an officer and gentleman. I was worried about joining a culture so far removed from what I had known. I loved the jungle, having been born and raised in that environment. My fellow former rebel commanders prevailed on me to accept the offer of commissionship.

I loved the teamwork developed among us officer candidates.

I went through the process of officer training. I breezed through the practical military exercises because, unlike my fellow officer candidates, I have had so much practice before. I learned to wear crisp military uniforms and when in formal gatherings, which fork to use first. When I was growing up, banana leaves to put food on and fingers for picking them up were sufficient. I learned to make my bed and keep my locker neat and organized. More importantly, I learned to value service again, but this time on the right side of the fence - with the duly constituted Armed Forces of the government.

It took a long time for me to internalize all the values of the Philippine Army. Yet, as I looked closer, I found many similarities with our own tribal army. On both sides, one relied on camaraderie, unity of command, superb combat leadership and courage to succeed. In both armies, there were willing volunteers, always ready to sacrifice their lives if necessary. Both armies claimed to be soldiers of the people. One army was outlawed; the other one was the official government army. It was a relief to receive the lieutenants' bar signifying my rank in the Army that is on the right side of the law!

Lieutenant Roberto Dumpao
Former top rebel field commander

A Dream Come True

I have always wanted to become a soldier. There was something about the military uniform that attracted me. There was also something about the bearing and the distinct manly decorum of the soldier that I always admired as a kid.

All that changed in the 1970s when young soldier grabbed my mother's precious *"malong."* That garment was rare and because ours was a royal Muslim family, we regarded it as disrespectful and an affront to our honor.

Wanting to take revenge for that rude act, I became a rebel.

I will never forget how those soldiers held us at gunpoint, accusing my entire family of being rebels. The frequent clashes between the troops and separatists caused extreme paranoia among the poorly-led soldiers who were desperately trying to corner enemies.

For more than two decades, I became their enemy.

My father did not actually approve of my becoming a rebel. I was barely fifteen years old, a second year high school student. But my sister was married to a fast-rising rebel commander. To avenge my mother's honor, he encouraged me to join him.

I had early dreams of becoming a soldier, although my rebel clan would
not approve of it.

At first, I was merely a part-time teenage rebel. I went to school
with my rifle. My teachers did not really mind that I missed several
classes and failed a few examinations. During those times that I was
absent, I participated in clashes against government troops. Before I
finished that school year, I had already been part of a few skirmishes.
My teachers still gave me passing grades despite my unexplained
absences.

My dangerous activities got my mother worried, so she asked a
local rebel commander to persuade me to finish school first.

"You should go to school because our revolution is going to last
for generations to come," was his practical advice. With the intensity
of fighting and the solid resistance of government forces against our
guerilla attacks, he must have realized that it was just a matter of
time until we also lost our young cause.

"You will not finish this struggle, so it is best that you should complete your studies, at least high school," he further advised.

I did not answer. I was a teenage guerilla and mighty proud of it. But my mother eventually prevailed. She got me to finish my last two years of high school. I sported extremely long hair — waist-length — and I brought my rifle to school. My principal allowed this and understood that there were days when I would be absent because I would be fighting government soldiers in a clash. That was my life as teenager.

In college, I dreamt of becoming a soldier again, because even while I was fighting government troops throughout high school, the desire to become a soldier never left me. I enrolled in advanced military subjects to acquire more knowledge formally. My instructors had no idea I was a veteran guerilla but I appreciated the things I did not learn as a rebel. I enjoyed the military drills, lessons on protocol and social graces and most of all military professionalism.

"I could not escape my long time desire of becoming a soldier," I told myself.

Actually, I sought admission to the Philippine Constabulary. I was so excited when I passed the entrance exams and the mandatory physical tests. But my past haunted me. Those processing my application found out about my past and promptly rejected it. I felt I had to let go of my dream. From then on, I just accepted the fact that I was not destined to become a soldier.

But Allah has His ways.

"Do you still want to become a military officer?" asked my rebel superior, I was dumbfounded because I had already given up.

"We will be integrating our senior commanders into the Armed Forces of the Philippines," he narrated.

We had the opportunity to join the ranks of the Armed Forces, our
archenemies for decades.

I knew we had been offered the opportunity to join the
Armed Forces as part of our peace agreement with the Philippine
government. I never imagined I would officially become a member
of the Armed Forces at the age of forty.

I was hesitant at first. It was just too good to be true! I could bring
along seventy of my followers who will also be integrated as enlisted
personnel. Most of them were also hesitant because they thought
that it might just be a trick, and that we would later be massacred.
Despite a signed peace process, our years as rebels in hiding did not
remove our instincts to always play it safe and consider the danger
of every move. But we just left it to the will of Allah and trusted the
agreement.

We were the first batch of "integrees" as we would later be called.

The Philippine military culture was a total shock.

We were trained to march in perfect step when we did not really practice military cadence in the mountains. We learned to salute our superiors, most of whom were too young to be even our sons. Many of us were "aged" warriors, seasoned in combat for years. Yet we forced ourselves to adjust especially to the strict regiment of formal camp life.

But our trainers, all of them Christians, had to adjust to us as well. No military camp in the Philippines had a mosque back then. Part of the peace agreement required the construction of a mosque where we trained. Our fellow trainees, some of whom had never met a Muslim before, had to learn and accept our ways. At times, they would not understand why we had to request to skip or miss a training activity because we had to pray so many times a day.

But our fellow trainees slowly learned and appreciated our cultural differences. When we said we could not eat pork, they did not insist. When we said that our religion forbade us to drink alcohol, they did not challenge that. When we said that we were devout Muslims, even the most religious Christians among them respected that. I felt wonderful.

For the first time, since the harmonious Christian-Muslim relationships were broken in the mid 1960's in Mindanao, we felt that there was a possibility that trust would be rebuilt again. We all graduated from the officer and candidate soldier training, fully respectful of our differences, yet mindful of our similarities.

Today, my batch mates are all members of different Philippine Army battalions. I have not heard of any gripes about how their lives have changed from separatist rebels to members of the Armed Forces.

I have forgotten the soldier who took my mother's prized garment. He was a part of the old Army culture, while I belong to the new, the enlightened Army culture.

Captain Jimmy Matalam
Moro National Liberation Front
rebel leader

Caught in the Crossfire

I was a foot soldier then and as such, probably experienced the worst difficulties imaginable. Looking back, I still do not understand why those events had to happen.

I grew up in the mountains, lived the rugged rural life and would probably still be living in my mountain village where I was born.

But the rebels came and what they told us made sense. At first, I was assigned menial tasks like carrying pots and pans. I understood that I needed to go through tests.

My first kill gave me a sense of liberation. Killing an unarmed but abusive person felt good. The movement affirmed this as it takes the law into its own hands, just to prove its relevance to the people.

Many did not believe that we could defeat the government.

"They are too strong and too many against you," the people said. Having heard that from the people several times, our leader went on a maniacal recruitment frenzy.

"There will be more rebels, than there are soldiers," one of our leaders boasted.

We trained as many recruits as we can in the ramp up of rebel strength.

Still lacking in rifles, we went for firearms-snatching missions. Whenever a policeman would be alone traveling home, we would point a gun at his temple and grab his firearm. If he resisted, we simply killed him. We also attacked militia detachments where we seized hundreds of high powered firearms. We also staged deadly ambushes against Army troops just so we could get their firearms and bloodied uniforms. Most importantly, we demanded the logging companies that operated in our zones to donate cash and firearms.

By 1983 we reached our peak in Cagayan, Apayao and Ilocos Norte. We had so much confidence in ourselves that we were staging daring raids at municipal halls, churches, schools, businesses and other targets. It was a display of raw power but our hubris eventually brought us defeat.

The military would not take our display of strength just like that. They fielded the Scout Rangers to directly confront us. While we can say we then had numerical superiority, we were told that their training was far superior to ours.

We were fighting the best troops of the Armed Forces, the Scout Rangers.

Working closely with the fighting Governor in Cagayan province, the Scout Rangers and other Army troops made life miserable for us. We suffered so many casualties during those years that many just gave up fighting. The military operations were just so intense that we often ran out of food, bullets and fighting spirit.

"You must undergo retraining," ordered our commander. He knew it. We, his troops were getting routed in the hands of the Army troopers.

We were sent to Marag Valley, the rebel bailiwick that was a world all its own.

Our own rebel teachers taught the people how to read and write. Of course, the first words they could write were revolutionary slogans. The school system was no longer running the government-approved curriculum. Instead, we implemented our own. Despite numerous defeats in other parts of the country, the survivors found renewed strength and vigor in this rebel-held village.

But our triumph would not last long. The military bombed our camp endlessly. The kids could not sleep. It was during this time that I realized how much the civilians were victimized by civil war. I could see elderly folks running around, confused whenever there was another artillery barrage. I also witnessed so many civilians die because of the bombings.

"Is it the government's fault or our own?" I thought to myself. Of course, my leaders would not entertain any doubts from fighters like me. Actually, there would have been more collateral damage in Marag, had there not been a cave where the people hid whenever be there were bombings and strafing.

I felt relieved when I was ordered to bring my troops to Ilocos Norte where we were to spend four years. I had gotten so tired of seeing civilians die that I felt I had to change environment. I also had enough of the mass evacuations of men, women, elderly and children into the forests and out of their homes.

"It is our fault," I concluded to myself.

"We should not be using the people as human shields in the first place," I murmured to myself.

Our world shrank further when the Armed Forces started organizing civilian militias in territories that were traditionally ours. They were locals who knew their villages well. They would report the presence of strangers like us. While we used to enjoy freedom of movement, we were suddenly constricted. When the military started using our former comrades who have since cooperated with the government to help hunt us, we knew we were going down.

Our camps like this were being routed one by one by highly-trained government forces.

In the face of intense military operations, many among us died and with every death, I started to believe that it was becoming more and more hopeless. Yet, it was impossible to leave because we were forbidden to do so. Many have escaped, sometimes bringing along their firearms. They were eventually punished and liquidated by our comrades. I did not want to suffer the same fate.

But one day, my wife, who was in the same group I belonged to, suggested that maybe could use our daughter's welfare as a reason for seeking permission to leave.

"We had left her with my in laws for five years," I explained to my commander.

"She just wants to see us and seek our consent," I lied to my commander.

Luckily, he obliged. And by using our daughter as an alibi, my wife and I finally set ourselves free.

We had since been living in peace since we left the movement in 1991. I have developed a deep respect for the relentless military operations that made me realize that we cannot win the war.

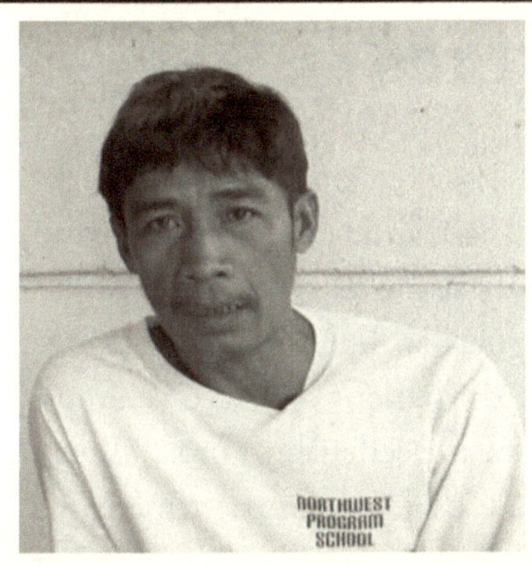

Mariano Calano
Rebel in Cagayan
from 1981 to 1991

Family Ties

My father was a principled man and, unlike others who collaborated with the Japanese invaders in World War II, he opted to become a guerilla. For the some strange reason, he never wanted to claim any of the benefits given to veterans. He said he fought for his country when it needed him most. There was no need to be paid for having done that. When the time came for us to rise to the challenges our generation faced, my father understood why his sons opted to become guerillas too.

I was only thirteen years old when I first joined protest marches. It was the right thing to do at that time.

We lived in an area of Manila where there were many informal settlers — one of the marginalized groups, under appreciated and often unemployed. They had the strongest motivation to protest. Our entire family led our urban poor neighbors in demanding their rights to decent housing and employment.

When Martial Law was declared, people were arrested, thrown to jail and even tortured. Two of my brothers immediately went underground. One became a member of the dreaded guerilla assassination squad, the Sparrow Unit. The other joined the communications department of the then outlawed Communist Party of the Philippines. I was left behind and became an activist, an organizer and speaker at mass protests.

It was easy to rally the urban poor to demand from the government.

What drove me to work full-time as an armed rebel hiding in the mountains was my subsequent arrest for possessing rebel propaganda material.

I thought they would kill me when I was picked up for distributing leaflets denouncing the government. It dawned on me that even legal struggles had no chance against the government. At 18, I volunteered to become a guerilla fighter — just like my father.

As I was leaving for my assignment up North, my two brothers suddenly gave up. Perhaps they feared for their lives. Perhaps they, too, realized that we may never win. As I began life as a guerilla fighter, one of my brothers who gave up, became a soldier. He was not just a regular soldier — he did intelligence work for the military and he was assigned to watch out for rebels like me. My father kept silent during those times.

I was assigned in the northern provinces of Isabela and Cagayan.
I distinctly recall one time when I was ordered to walk hundreds of
kilometers through the peaks of the Sierra Madre mountains. On
December 31, 1980, New Years' Eve, we reached the boundary of
Isabela and Cagayan. We got there amid exploding fire crackers, and
noise making — that ushered me into the colorful life I would lead
in Isabela.

Inspite of the fact that Isabela was one of the first guerilla
regions organized upon the founding of the rebellion in 1969, it
never really took off because the pioneers were reassigned to open
more rebel fronts. I helped build the Isabela guerilla organization.

I loved leading the peasants who joined the rebellion.

Inspired by pure idealism and conviction that the armed struggle
could win, I poured all my youthful energies into training our recruits.
Given my previous activist work in Manila and the supportive family
dinner conversations we had, I was the most experienced among my
comrades. I was one of the youngest party councilors at the tender
age of 23.

After a few years in the mountains, I decided to visit my family.

I wanted to pay a visit to my parents, who were taking care of my jobless wife and two kids while I spent my years in the jungle.

I was almost as young as the people I was leading when I was picked as a leader in my 20's.

It would have been a happy reunion, but my soldier brother decided to have me arrested on that day when all I wanted was to share stories with them.

"How is your life in the military," I asked him.

"Fine," he said. "How is your life in the mountains?" he shot back. As he was about to finish his sentence, a caravan of vehicles arrived. I couldn't move nor escape because I was holding my young child in my arms.

"Do not resist arrest, brother," my brother said. Most heavily affected was our father, who was extremely bothered that one of his sons would turn against another. He hasn't quite forgiven my brother after that.

I was later placed under house arrest. But sensing that often, more sinister plots were afoot, I escaped and fled to Isabela, leaving my wife once more.

I was no longer a trusted party member after that. I understood why they already replaced me as commander. They did that to all who had been arrested. I got a demotion, even if I did not disclose any details. The Party members no longer trusted me. They pulled out my few remaining troops without consulting me. They did not even invite me to the new camp, though I was just in the vicinity. Then I began to understand what my brother meant whenever he talked about respect. My brother had contracted tuberculosis, and, like my father who refused to claim benefits as a veteran, he did not seek treatment in any government facility.

My leaders in the rebel movement began distrusting me after
I got arrested.

"I did not become a guerilla for the benefits that I would get," he used to say. "I wanted to become a guerilla because I wanted to serve."

My comrades' baseless accusations and the way they treated

me after my arrest showed they had lost respect for me, despite the years I served the movement. I wrote a very angry letter which they ignored.

It pained me to be distrusted by my comrades. But as days turned into months, more and more deep penetration agents sent by the military were discovered and summarily executed. I did not wait to test my luck. I voluntarily surrendered to my brother, but this time with the full blessing of my entire family.

On that day in 1992 our family was reunited again after twenty years.

Rolando V. Lee
Rebel leader in Isabela
in the 1980s

An Ordinary Fugitive

I joined the rebellion for a purely personal reason: I had just escaped from prison and I needed an efficient cover.

Nothing in my background would indicate any interest in becoming a rebel. I was born so poor that I did not even finish grade one. I was eleven years old when I started working as a husk gatherer, earning me 60 centavos per day. I made money for food toiling this way for several years.

Life was hard. I had a good voice, so I was often asked to go with the groups serenading women. That was when I discovered my natural interest in leading a stowaway's life. I was a happy-go-lucky teenager when I discovered that one of my siblings was working in a construction site in Tanay, Rizal. I followed him there until I got laid off. Between jobs, one of the workers asked me to join their union. That started three decades of involvement with the underground.

During my first months with the revolution, my comrades taught me how to read and write. Each time we went somewhere and stopped, my buddies would teach me how to write. I could write now, though my spelling is often incorrect. I have to thank my early comrades for that.

To gain the trust of the farmers, we helped them in the farms.

During my first decade of the revolution, I appreciated the beauty and relevance of the ideology. I actually learned how to care for people as a young rebel. We offered to help the people with anything we could - burning forest clearings for crop planting, pulling out grass and weeds. We did everything so that the citizens would trust us as their true defenders.

The people reciprocated our kindness. Everything we had, whatever we ate, the small money we had, the toiletries we used, were all from the people. Back then, I honestly felt that they loved us.

We never asked about each other's past. That was convenient for me because I had a dark secret. My wife committed suicide and I was blamed for it. I was sent to prison, almost went mad thinking of what might happen to our children. After a few months, I was taken off maximum security and allowed to run errands for the prison guard. That was when I escaped. At first, I did not know where to run until I remembered that my friends from the union might know somebody who can give me sanctuary. They directed me to the New Peoples' Army.

Barely able to read and write, I was made to appreciate the propaganda that we spread. The standard line was that the government was heading nowhere and had no interest in protecting the citizens. We taught them how to hate and condemn, without carefully evaluating the factors that caused the situation. I felt like a hypocrite preaching the value of justice and the rule of law when I was actually a fugitive from the same law!

Barely able to read and write, I was already spreading our critical view of the government to the people.

I did not question discrepancies between what was said and done. But in my mind, I wondered why we did not have second thoughts about asking them to support us even when they barely earned enough for their own need or why we called ourselves their protectors when we often used them as human shields whenever we were 'cornered' during military operations.

I never complained as the movement gave me the perfect cover — a very convenient one. While my case was still pending, I knew I was in for decades, with the slow pace of justice in the Philippines.

Thus, I decided to simply survive and watch events unfold. The stowaway attitude ruled again.

Times were difficult during the height of the insurgency in the 1980's. The Army was on the offensive and we clearly were at a disadvantage. There were times when we had clashes before breakfast, right before lunch and before dinner- one firefight for every meal. The Armed Forces would comb the mountains to track us down. We ran, we escaped, but some died, and many of them were left in the battlefields.

What I could not handle then were the times when we were submerged in water and wet all night and all day. We slept even when we were wet, hungry, lacked sleep and tired. But again, I had no right to complain. This was a better life than the cold floor of the prison cell.

While I had every reason to stay as a rebel, the youth that we recruited had no reason to. Some of them led privileged lives. Unlike some of us, true sons of the earth who have not known even the basic comforts in life, these young students were bred and raised well. I would silently pray whenever one would fall in a firefight with the Army. That is one less life that could have made the Philippines a better place — if only other options were open. But the armed struggle then was the only choice to fight the dictatorial government. While I did not embrace the ideology, I did not disagree with them. I was a rebel because I needed to run from the law while these young students who had better choices in life were there for the ideals.

Long walks through the jungles and other physical work required of us did not tire me out.

It was the false front I had to keep and the growing awareness that I was not the only one like that in the movement.

We were just fooling the people we sought to serve.

We promised to give them lands through our land reform program but in secret meetings, we agreed to withhold these sweeping grants.

"They might get contented too soon," declared our commander.

We promised not to take away anything from them. But in the aftermath of the total log ban in the early 1990's which cut the illicit support of the loggers, we faced hard times. Thus, we devised all schemes to make money. It was actually during those lean times that we systematized the now infamous revolutionary tax system.

I also got tired because people showed signs of rebellion fatigue. The changes we promised them never came. The projects we pledged to do, did not materialize. It seemed that we had just been playing with their hearts and minds during the years that we totally influenced them. They soon got tired of supporting us when they realized there were other ways.

I too got tired and resolved to face the cases filed against me. I surrendered to authorities and after a few years, my name was finally cleared. My days as a fugitive were over and I no longer needed to pretend to be a rebel.

Romeo Sambajon
Rebel team leader in Rizal

An Abductee, Not a Rebel

I was a United Methodist church pastor on fire. I particularly enjoyed running alternative learning systems classes in farflung barangays. I liked opening a kindergarten school in an inaccessible village. Just seeing the kids enjoy learning the alphabet was pure joy for me.

The cadre of the city-based front organizations of the rebel armed group must have spotted my overzealous energy. One of their leaders soon asked me to speak in rallies, decrying the lack of support for education. I spoke with passion because I owned the frustration. I knew that the lack of classrooms stunted the desire of children to learn. I knew what the lack of teachers in remote villages meant to the long term future. Slowly, I was being convinced that only through revolution can the prioritization of education be effected. I was naive and I believed them.

"Books, not guns and bullets, should be the priority of the government," they would say over and over. Though I was fast becoming sympathetic to their cause, I never imagined becoming a member of the underground New People's Army. I believed in God, worked for God and served the people as an agent of God. But the rebels had other plans for me.

They literally abducted me to become a full-time rebel.

In 2007, the cadres invited me to speak about humanitarian law before village officials. By then, I was also considered an expert on this topic. But the rebels deceived me.

I was just invited to enlighten village officials when the rebels abducted me to become a full-time fighter.

In that lakeside village in Lake Buhi in Camarines Sur, two armed men accosted me. They then blindfolded me as they led me to a motorboat.

"Where are you taking me?" I panicked. "You will be safe, and there is no need to worry," they casually told me.

We walked farther inland after we docked on the other side of the lake. I kept praying that I will not be harmed.

When they removed my blindfold after what seemed an eternity walking through dense and humid forest, I saw the "red fighters," as the armed rebel regulars called themselves. I was inside their secret camp!

I saw familiar faces among these leaders of that gathering of about a hundred guerillas. They were all in the rallies where they often invited me to speak.

"I thought you just wanted me to teach a 4-day course in that village," I asked them. One of the leaders smirked.

"From now on, you can't go down anymore. You have been seen by soldiers as we brought you here," he told me. I knew that he was lying but still I entertained the possibility.

"And if the soldiers learned you have joined us, they will kill you," he said. His face was totally serious, just the mark of an expert propagandist.

"I still have to officiate a wedding in our church tomorrow," I protested. He did not want to hear anymore of it.

"Don't worry. From now on, your family will receive eight thousand pesos, one sack of rice and groceries monthly," he assured me. I thought about my family. My wife was from the indigenous tribe and our kids were still small. Caring for small kids and doing menial work will not sustain my family. What if they did not give them the allowance they promised?

I finished the course in 45 days. By that time, my family must have gone crazy looking for me. My congregation must have also been completely puzzled by my unexplained disappearance. I would soon learn through our couriers that my bishop and my district superintendent desperately looked for me. When they learned that I had gone to the rebel side, they were thoroughly disappointed.

I did not like the life of an armed rebel. I was totally against the use of guns and violence. More than that, I hated the way we lived off poor rural folk.

I particularly pitied the owners of small stores who could hardly make ends meet. On a monthly basis, we required them to give us a kilo of sugar, 50 grams of coffee, 2 packs of cigarettes, sardines, bars of soap, rice and salt. Every time we took away our goods, the store would be half empty. I do not know how the small entrepreneurs ever managed to replenish their stocks. But the following month, when it was time again to collect, they would grudgingly part with the goods again. I did not like that. In fact, I was ashamed because I was still a pastor, first and foremost.

I really did not know why because back when I was still in the city, I knew that the revolutionary tax collectors amassed a lot. It was the talk of the town an engineer of one of the telecom companies building a cellsite there pissed in his pants when rebels suddenly appeared in his tower site. Just like all project contractors, he quickly gave the money.

But what bothered me was that there seemed to be no projects for which the money was collected. The collectors often said that the money would be used to construct projects for the rural folk — schools, water systems, clinics and roads in the villages. But none of these seemed forthcoming.

I became even more ashamed when I realized that the rural folk had no money to give us. Instead, we got rice and chicken from them. This was the exact opposite of what we say when we introduce them to our belief systems.

I asked permission to leave, but was repeatedly denied.

"You could rest if you want, but we must take your fourteen year old child in your place," our commander declared. I was a father and that was unthinkable for me. So I went on with my work.

I attempted to be freed from the hard life of the guerilla several times.

The greatest blessing from God came when I was captured by military agents. I did not resist. In fact, deep inside me, I welcomed being captured. I was finally free.

I was devastated when I saw my family after a few years. My wife was so thin. She was severely malnourished. My children did not recognize me anymore. They did not even want to approach me. They were all thin, hungry and pale.

Our house was totally dilapidated. None of the things I saved for remained.

"Where did our things go?" I asked my wife.

"I sold them because you did not come home. What will your children eat?" answered my wife.

Then it dawned on me that, not one centavo of the promised eight thousand peso monthly allowance came after all those long months. I cried in front of my family. I caused all their misery.

I have since rebuilt my family. I am happy now and will remain so for as long as I stay away from the rebels.

Edwin Nazarinonda
Pastor turned rebel in Bicol

REBEL STORIES

A Former Terrorist Speaks

I am Corporal Ashrey Abtahi of the Philippine Army. My job is to secure, drive around and guide visiting military officers in the city of Zamboanga. I usually engage in a casual conversation with guests. They often ask about me and my previous assignments in the Army. They are shocked when I tell them that I used to be with the Abu Sayyaf Group or ASG, widely regarded as terrorists.

An incredulous officer once asked, "So, a former kidnapper is driving me around?" I felt his discomfort—or perhaps even fear. "Yes, sir!" I answered politely. More than ten years ago, I decided I wanted drastic change in my life, so I turned against my comrades when I agreed to testify against them. I am aware that my story is so unusual and difficult to believe.

My father was a militia man, an armed forces auxiliary in Santa Cruz, Davao del Sur. He and my mother were both from Talipao town, the "terrorist haven" of Sulu. They escaped the heavy fighting in our province in the early 1970s to join the mass exodus of Muslims from the conflict zones. Like the rest of our relatives who migrated from our war torn island province, we joined one of the numerous pockets of Muslim communities in predominantly Christian towns.

It was not easy for us to start life in this new town. Poor and jobless, my father volunteered to become part of the militia. His job did not pay well, but it was enough to buy rice. I was twelve years old when he died in an ambush by the communist-inspired rebels in 1986.

My mother considered staying in Davao del Sur. She had gotten used to it and wanted to raise us there. But her relatives in Sulu prevailed. The elders on both sides of the clan requested that we return. Against her wishes, we moved back.

This was the time *Alhakatul Al-Islamiyya* or the Abu Sayyaf Group was sweeping our town for recruits. Many of the first leaders of the group had large clans and followers in our town. Their families even owned vast idle agricultural lands there. They were able to win over many recruits because of family ties and strong religious influence.

At that time, our group was a radical version of our separatist brothers in the Moro National Liberation Front. The big difference was the strong emphasis on the religious basis of our holy war.

My relatives were already full time members of the Abu Sayyaf Group, so I also joined them. In fact, I was already allowed to attend their meetings.

A religious or community leader would preside over those meetings. He would recite verses from the Quran that referred to our struggle. They always emphasized the fight against the non-believers of Allah. They explained why the jihad was necessary and encouraged all able-bodied male and female members of our community to carry arms for Allah.

I became an active member of the group in 1999 and had my first terrorist training near our village. "We all want you to become our Holy warriors," our trainer began. "You must first devote yourselves to the study of the Quran," he continued. I expected intense military training. Instead, we were steeped in the teachings of the Quran.

A community leader presided over our jihadist training.

"We want you to become *mujahideen*, or the soldiers of Allah," our main teacher would say. As the days went by, intense Islamic study continued and I realized that we were not being trained to fight but to become martyrs.

"You must be ready to fight for our cause anytime," we were told. As I understood it then, our main task was to spread the word of the Quran first to our brothers who were unable to read.

I did not know how we were to defeat those who did not believe in Allah. All I knew was that we justified our need to make money so that we can buy more firearms to strengthen our cause. It was explained to us that using the money for purposes other than strengthening the group was against the Quran.

I graduated from the Place of the Martyrs (*Darushohada*) School in Talipao, Sulu along with sixty other new recruits in 1999. "Go on and be Martyrs for Allah," said the Abu Sayyaf commander, with whom I was to work closely later on. He was known as Commander Global, the inspiring Muslim scholar highly regarded for his combat leadership skills.

"Your task is to teach the Quran to our potential recruits," he told me. Introducing the Quran to illiterate recruits was much tougher than pulling the trigger on non-believers. My first engagements were very challenging but I took my task seriously. I really believed that I was a martyr. I passed the first test of Commander Global, who then made me run errands at first, but later became his trusted assistant.

All of young recruits, started out ignorant of our cause.

"Make sure you check our intelligence agents in the villages," my mentor would say. Our trusted informers in the villages were about my age and I think I connected with them because I was friendly.

"Let us know if there are military operations," I instructed the teenagers who served as spies, couriers and later, our recruits.

"We are your protectors," I would tell the village elders we had summoned for meetings.

"You must feed us when we are here with you," I reminded them. The villagers were used to fighting since the 1900s when the Americans tried to conquer us. Warrior groups were familiar to the villagers and we, the Tausugs, were just the latest among a long line of fighters.

I would say I was inspired and was ready to play my role as a martyr—until we engaged in a series of high-profile kidnappings involving both locals and foreigners. Easiest to kidnap were the locals, owners of hardware stores and similar businesses in Zamboanga City, whose relatives we demanded to deposit an amount we had agreed upon in one of our bank accounts. We held our captive until we confirmed the deposit. Releasing our victim took a day or two.

Tourists in posh resorts, especially those in the island of Palawan nearby or even in Sabah, Malaysia, fetched higher prices but such kidnapping operations required more planning and resources. We started with a number of outriggers. Commander Global would plan the operation, along with other top Abu Sayyaf commanders. Each operation was planned to the very last detail: we would carry out plans at high tide, know how many guards each resort had, routes safest from Malaysian and Philippine patrol boats. During the first few operations, I took part in the planning stage but was never involved in the kidnapping operations because I had no gun of my own back then. That was why whenever Commander Global would justify such kidnappings by saying that we needed the money to buy arms, I believed him.

One daring adventure was the kidnapping they pulled off in Sipadan, Malaysia in 2001. They brought back foreigners into our heavily fortified secret camp.

"Please have pity on us," begged the Caucasian hostages. Knowing that they were on vacation mode at the time they were kidnapped, we knew that putting them through physical pain may be enough to have them convince their relatives to pay up fast.

We used the ransom money we collected to buy us firearms and uniforms.

"We will raise the money," they would say after each beating. Indeed, money came from each of the victims' relatives. I was given sixty thousand pesos which was part of the entire ransom amount paid by the family of a foreigner we later released. I used the money to buy an MI6 rifle equipped with a grenade launcher. I became part of major kidnapping operations afterwards.

During my first mission, I still believed that we needed the money we earned from kidnappings so we could recruit more holy warriors. I never doubted that then because I was close to the most respected Abu Sayyaf commander of the time. I still have memories of times when I would read the Quran quietly beside cages full of hostages.

"We are here because it is the will of Allah and not for the money or anything else," I would remind the newer Abu Sayyaf members. I believed that we were a group of mujahideen tasked to destroy non-believers.

I began to have doubts that eventually eroded my personal commitment when we began to execute more daring, high-yield kidnappings and lots of ransom money came pouring in. At that point, we earned the label "terrorists." For those who still believed that we were holy warriors, it was disappointing to know that we were regarded as nothing more than a band of bandits who contributed to the rapidly deteriorating image of the country. I also noticed that some of our most devout leaders have also been seduced by money. They had become extravagant gift-givers and even "Robin Hoods" in their communities. They would dole out money until their pockets were empty and it was time once more to kidnap.

I probably would have continued taking part in the kidnappings if we hadn't been captured in a posh resort in Eastern Mindanao during a botched operation. One of our planners made a mistake in calculating when low tide would come. We went in, unaware that in the direction we took, the sea bottom was full of corals. We got stuck when the tide was low and the resort guards fired at us. We escaped by commandeering another boat and when it ran out of fuel, we had to dock. Luckily, a Muslim community there provided temporary refuge and allowed us to leave our firearms. So as not to raise suspicions, we left the community no longer as a group but as individuals.

I was eventually captured when I attempted to go back to retrieve the firearms we left in their care. My whole world crumbled when I was imprisoned. I felt as if all the youthful energy that drove me before my capture left my body.

A few days later, an official asked me, "Do you want to turn witness against your comrades?" It did not take long for me to decide. At that time disillusionment has crept in already. I began to ask myself whether we were really martyrs and holy warriors because the rest of the country seemed to see us differently. To many of our countrymen, we were nothing more than despicable terrorists.

I felt so uneasy on the first hearing I testified against my former comrades. I feared that the Abu Sayyaf would wipe out my entire family. I have witnessed them torture or worse, behead hostages whose families were unable to pay the ransom we demanded. I also knew what they could do to my family.

I am convinced that turning against my comrades is right.

Eventually, my entire family was relocated to a safer place. I have since married and I now have a child. I still fear for my life but now, I am free to live and think my own thoughts. I am no longer a slave to hypocrisy the way I was when I was a terrorist.

Ashrey Abtahi
Former Abu Sayyaf terrorist

Coup 'd etat Veteran

"May God bless you all," I bid goodbye to my troops. I was then the First Sergeant of the 12th Scout Ranger Company in Davao in 2003. As, the highest ranking non-commissioned officer in the unit, I made sure to speak before troops jumped off to every combat operation. It was standard operating procedure for every Scout Ranger First Sergeant to do so. But, this time, my troops were not going to another jungle combat operation. They were going to the capital city of Manila to seize and control a posh hotel in the hope of pushing the woman President to resign.

"Sir with all due respect, I do not think you will succeed," I politely approached my commanding officer.

"Do not worry, First Sergeant," he remarked back.

"I will take care of our troops," he continued.

"Just take care of those who are left behind!" He continued.

I have seen that headstrong stance a few times before. In fact, my commanding officer's remarks were similar to the way my former officers behaved in the First Scout Ranger Regiment displayed before, 15 years ago.

It was the first time that my commanding officer and the select number of troops that volunteered to join him got involved in a clandestine attempt to stage a military coup 'd etat against the incumbent President.

"Sir your move is compromised. Our intelligence units already know of your moves," I almost pleaded for him to reconsider.

He did not budge. His mind was set. He had to execute the bold plan together with several hundred others from different elite units of the Armed Forces.

"Nothing will happen sir. You won't win," I made my final remark.

"I respect your recommendation, First Sergeant, but please respect my decision," he told me flatly. And off they boarded for Manila. I was speaking from experience when I told my commanding officer that they won't win. After all, I had been an active participant in one major bloody coup 'd etat attempt and a few less violent ones before that. I knew what I was talking about because I have gone through the full cycle, from planning to execution and later, remorse. Together with hundreds of others who had seen the face of terror as we battled against our fellow men in uniform, I suffered through it all.

The siege of Makati in November 1989 was the worst that I went through. I was then a Sergeant handling the Centurions, the Scout Ranger Class 100-89, at the Scout Ranger Training School in Fort Magsaysay, Nueva Ecija. The students were volunteers from the different Armed Forces units who have made it a goal to get the coveted Scout Ranger tab. To wear the badge was a status symbol.

Each of our students wanted it so bad, that they were willing to do anything to get it. We made them run long distances under the heat of the tropical sun. We had the students go through the most intensive marksmanship training. Yet, nobody seemed to know the grand design for the class, except for the school commandant.

"We are going to Manila for a mission," he declared. I did not understand what he meant. All, I knew was that he had credibility because he had been a key participant in the bloodless people's revolution in EDSA in 1986.

I do not think the Scout Ranger students understood the cryptic tone of his briefing. But those who had been

I was a Scout Ranger trainer when the coup in 1989 happened.

through the previous series of coup attempts in 1987, knew what the commandant meant.

"We are going for another round again," they murmured to themselves.

Contrary to popular belief that rebels are all ideology-driven, we definitely were not. Though some of us had gripes and grumblings about the administration in the late 1980's, these were not really heavy enough to stake our careers for, yet there was something in the camaraderie in elite military units that almost compelled us to go where all our buddies led us. In the time-honored tradition of standing up for each other, we did not let anyone down whenever he needed us.

"Our country needs reform, and we are being called upon to act," exhorted our commandant.

"All it takes for evil to triumph is for good men to do nothing," he further motivated us. He portrayed us as the good men, out to save the Philippines from doom.

There is something in the camaraderie of elite units that unites us through thick and thin.

Our Scout Ranger students could not believe their eyes when they saw us, their trainers, packing for what is now regarded as the bloodiest coup 'd etat attempt in the history of the Philippines.

The Centurions were off to their test mission to liberate the country from evil.

While others took control of key skyscrapers in the business district of Makati, we were tasked to attack and take control of the police headquarters in Camp Crame. We were first consolidated at the business district adjacent to the police camp. As we were assembled to attack, heavy fire fights between us and the defenders of the camp ensued.

"We do not have to fight each other," we heard our fellow soldiers attacking us. We knew then that they were defending themselves against our attacks. But our messianic complex was so strong that we felt we had the right to shoot and even kill, our fellow soldiers defending the flag.

We may have had fighting spirit, we were simply out numbered by the defenders of the camp. We soon reassembled, dressed in civilian clothes and prepared to abandon everything.

We first hid our weapons and extricated ourselves from the area. We knew we were about to be arrested, and we used the evasion skills we learned at the Scout Ranger Training School to avoid detention. We made our way out, and hid for several months. Our entire unit was disbanded after that.

"What do we do now?" asked my wife. My family depended on my Ranger's salary for our existence. I did not know what to do. I started blaming our school commandant for putting us in harm's way. My fellow Scout Rangers shared the same sentiment. We were so desperate for help, yet our officers were all detained. Nobody could help the hundreds of enlisted personnel like me, regain our careers.

"Would you accept a demotion of two ranks and for you to pay the firearm that you lost?" asked the court martial judge. We regarded the leniency offered to us to remain in the service and accept the punishment fair.

All of us nodded in approval, knowing that our families would suffer with our decision.

"It is better than spending time in jail," another one remarked.

Everybody agreed and our group, a proud group of battle-seasoned Scout Rangers, were demoted two ranks. What was harder to accept however, was the change in lifestyle brought on by our decreased income and payments for the firearms we lost.

"We can only afford to eat three decent meals a day," declared my wife. For the three years I had to serve that punishment, we had no extras: no snacks, zero luxuries, even my child had to bear all that. We could barely afford to send her to school. Yet, we managed to scrimp during those years.

The difficulties of coping with reduced finances were the biggest challenges my wife and I faced. Yet, through it all, we suffered together. Gone was the school commandant who promised to take care of us, no matter what. Gone was the group of civilians who, in secret meetings, promised all the support they can give. We only had our families — our spouses, who endured the repercussions of our decisions.

"Would you like to join this coup attempt in Manila?" asked our former school commandant who, since that harrowing experience had reinvented himself as an elected official in the Philippines. He was at it again, using the same charms he used on us more than a decade ago. And the gleam in the eyes of the young company commanders, one of whom was my own commander, showed he was going to sway them through the dangerous path that he led us to years before. They also entertained the idea of reforming our country. I heard the same response.

I will never allow myself and my fellow soldiers be tricked by destabilization recruiters again. That is me in the white shirt.

"This is for our country," young officers in our battalion explained their recruitment pitch. Most of the enlisted men, just like me before, joined out of loyalty to these inspiring young combat officers.

"Come back if you still can," I advised them as they set out. But I knew that just like me before, there was no turning back for a warrior under this idealistic spell.

Predictably, my men, including our officers, all went to jail for the failed military coup 'd etat. Just like us before, their families endured the pains of punishment and were torn apart by shifting loyalties when everybody is sent to detention.

After a short five years, most of them came back to serve again. And just like me, none of them would have anything to do with military adventurism again.

Master Sergeant (retired) Victor Hilado
Former military rebel

ACKNOWLEDGEMENTS

I wish to thank the people that made this book possible. The Scout Rangers who shared their personal stories deserve my most profuse thanks.

I deeply acknowledge the support of my leaders BGen. Eduardo Davalan, Col. Ramon Yogyog, Col. Glen Paje, Col. Ted Llamas and Ltc. Armand Arevalo.

I wish to thank my buddies at the Task Group Panther who gave me the perfect field writing environment. Special thanks go to my 4th Scout Ranger Company buddies and other members of the combat test mission control group that I commanded as I wrote this book.

I wish to thank the rebel photographers whose images we captured in our raids of their secret camps. I have shared the works of these unnamed rebel photographers throughout this book.

I also thank my team composed of Erwin Agustin, Herwin Barbado, Tony Relao, Zaldy Liban, Bryan Cañedo, Leo Salinel and Analyn Aurelio for their effort and sacrifice to make this book happen.

Many thanks to Ms. Tin Bartolome for editing this book.

Most of all, I thank my family - wife Jing, mother Nelia, daughters Deji and Jamina and son Rafi.

Lieutenant Colonel Dennis V. Eclarin